# The Farmer's Wife
# Cookie
# Cookbook

## OVER 250 BLUE-RIBBON RECIPES

### LELA NARGI, EDITOR

Voyageur Press

First published in 2009 by Voyageur Press, an imprint of MBI Publishing Company, 400 First Avenue North, Suite 300, Minneapolis, MN 55401 USA

Voyageur Press titles are also available at discounts in bulk quantity for industrial or sales-promotional use. For details write to Special Sales Manager at MBI Publishing Company, 400 First Avenue North, Suite 300, Minneapolis, MN 55401 USA.

To find out more about our books, visit us online at www.voyageurpress.com.


Editor: Melinda Keefe
Designer: Lois Stanfield

Printed in China

Library of Congress Cataloging-in-Publication Data
 The Farmer's wife's cookie cookbook : over 250 blue-ribbon recipes! / Lela Nargi.
— 1st ed.
    p. cm.
 Includes bibliographical references.
 ISBN 978-0-7603-3513-0 (comb-plc)
 1. Cookies. I. Nargi, Lela. II. Farmer's wife.
 TX772.F372 2009
 641.8'654—dc22
                    2008044266

**Editor Lela Nargi** is a writer who lives in Brooklyn, New York. She is the author of *Around the Table: Women on Food, Cooking, Nourishment, Love . . . and the Mothers Who Dished It Up for Them* and *Knitting Lessons: Tales from the Knitting Path*. She is also the editor of *Knitting Memories: Reflections on the Knitter's Life*, *Knitting Through It: Inspiring Stories for Times of Trouble*, *The Farmer's Wife Baking Cookbook*, and *The Farmer's Wife Comfort Food Cookbook*, all published by Voyageur Press.

# Contents

# Introduction
## Making Cookies with *The Farmer's Wife*

The *Farmer's Wife* was a monthly magazine published in Minnesota between the years 1893 and 1939. In an era long before the Internet and high-speed travel connected us all, the magazine aimed to offer community among hardworking rural women by providing a forum for their questions and concerns, and assistance with the day-to-day goings-on about the farm— everything from raising chickens and slaughtering hogs, to managing scant funds and dressing the children, to keeping house and running the kitchen.

The farmer's wife was, most assuredly, a cookie maker. She made cookies when there was no real occasion at all—just to keep the cookie jar full or to pack a sweet treat for a school lunch box—and she made cookies, many *many* cookies, during the holiday season. She also made sweet finger foods aplenty for the formal and casual tea parties and coffee klatches she hosted in her living room and at her kitchen table. The scope of these treats

extended beyond what we think of as specifically "the cookie," and that is why recipes for gingerbread, bars and squares, and also fried goodies like doughnuts appear on these pages. This book is organized by the intention of *The Farmer's Wife*—to offer sweet snacks to any and all comers throughout the day—rather than any strict adherence to a textbook definition of a cookie.

Curiously, cookie making seems to have been such a mundane and informal activity for the farmer's wife that she scarcely needed recipes to see her through. Oftentimes, she must just have whipped up a few batches from whatever ingredients she had in the cupboard, or baked or fried up leftover pastry scraps from some other kitchen undertaking. Cookie making was a relatively casual procedure, one not riddled with secrets—like cake or pie baking, which required article upon article in the magazine over the years that expounded upon methods for achieving the moistest crumb, the smoothest frosting, the most delicate pie crust, the perfectly perky filling. So, cookie recipes from the magazine here are supplemented with adaptations of recipes from other collections—most notably from the excellent *Pennsylvania Dutch Cook Book* by Ruth Hutchison (for many farmers' wives came from this tradition), and also several rural church and community compilations, which are similar in spirit to the magazine itself. These are mostly simple, no-nonsense, old-fashioned cookies—satisfying standbys of the country kitchen cookie jar, sweet but modest offerings to gladden the hearts of a hard-working family.

The recipes have been reprinted here as closely as possible to how they originally ran. Many were sent in by the magazine's own readers, and they reflect highly individual methods of instruction and notions about what, in cookie making, could be considered common sense and therefore necessitating no instruction at all.

In their language, they reflect the curious style and manners of their times, and herein lies a great deal of their charm, and the reason I have tried to alter them as little as possible. Anyone accustomed to reading cookbooks will feel right at home among the pages of this book. After all, the farmer's wife was nothing if not matter-of-fact, and so were her recipes. Anyone new to cookbooks, and more particularly, historical cookbooks, is advised to follow the golden rule of the recipe: read it thoroughly, start to finish and preferably more than once, before embarking. Make sure you understand the instructions and the order in which they are to be carried out; make sure you have all the ingredients at hand and assembled; and make sure to preheat your oven for a good 20 to 30 minutes before you are ready to bake.

Wherever possible, I have attempted to abolish confusing, misleading, or laborious instructions. I've also substituted modern equivalents for obsolete measurements like the gill (4 ounces) and the teacup (8 ounces). More than anything, this book wants to be used, not merely perused and admired. So, please use it! And know that as you do, you are baking up a bit of farmland history.

ALL READY FOR Christmas Overseas!

# Read This First

## How to Use This Book

The farmer's wife always sifted her flour once before measuring. However, this instruction is now pretty much obsolete, since most contemporary flours are sifted before they are packed. When measuring, level off flour in the cup unless otherwise directed.

Some recipes in this book approximate flour measurements or give a wide range (say, from 3–6 cups). The farmer's wife was inclined to mix all other ingredients before adding enough flour to make a dough of the thickness she required. The amount of flour necessary can vary according to weather, altitude, and type of flour used, and a baker who can remain a little flexible about measurements in these instances will have greater success in the final result.

Unless otherwise specified, use large eggs when eggs are called for in a recipe.

1 square Baker's chocolate refers to the 1-ounce variety.

Rolled oats should be of the old-fashioned type, not the quick cooking.

**Measuring Equivalents:**
1 pint = 2 c.
1 quart = 4 c.

**1 pound yields:**

Sifted all-purpose flour—4 c.

Sifted cake flour—4½ c.

Graham flour—3½ c.

Cornmeal—3 c.

Rolled oats—5½ c.

White sugar—2¼ c.

Brown sugar—2½ c.

Powdered sugar—2¾ c.

Molasses and honey—1⅓ c.

Milk—2 c.

Nutmeats—4 c., chopped

Dried fruit—3 c.

# KEEP THE OLD STONE CROCK WHERE THE CHILDREN CAN REACH IT

By Annette C. Dimock, *April 1924*

A cooky is jolly in its very name! I wonder—is this new and changing generation getting away from the old-time sentiment clinging around the word "cooky" and the thought of Mother's and Grandmother's or Aunty's or Big Sister's cooky jar?

Have cooky sheets cut to fit the oven. Russia iron is the first choice, heavy tin the second. Such sheets are kept in better condition and give better results if instead of being greased they are rubbed very lightly with paraffin. If kept absolutely clean, they will require no greasing.

# Drop Cookies

These are the easiest cookies in the farmer's wife's arsenal. Simply mix, drop, and bake. Even small children can help with making these, and older children, allowed to whip up batches on their own, will feel ever-so-confident in their baking abilities.

## ❦ Jam Marguerites

*Perhaps the fastest, simplest cookies of all time.*

| | |
|---|---|
| 2 egg whites | 3 tbsp. raspberry or other jam |
| 2 drops lemon extract | Saltine- or Ritz-type crackers |

Beat egg whites stiff and gradually add the jam. Mix until thoroughly blended. Add lemon extract. Place by the spoonful on crackers and sprinkle with more nuts. Bake at 350°F until delicately brown.

*Variation:*
Black Walnut Crisps: Substitute 6 tbsp. chopped black walnuts for jam, and vanilla for lemon extract; add 6 tbsp. sugar.

## ❦ Marshmallow Marguerites

| | |
|---|---|
| 1 egg white | ½ c. nuts, chopped |
| ½ c. marshmallows, cut up | Saltine- or Ritz-type crackers |

Beat egg white till stiff. Add marshmallows and nuts. Mix. Drop small spoonfuls of mixture on individual crackers and bake at 350°F until a glaze has formed on top. Serve strictly fresh.

*Plain drop cookies are not easy to come by with the farmer's wife—she preferred nuts or molasses in hers, or sour cream to replace the butter. The following two recipes are adapted from* Our Favorite Recipes, *a church collection from New Jersey, for those days when you must bake but there's very little in the larder.*

## ❦ Plain Drop Cookies

½ c. unsalted butter, softened     2¼ c. flour
1 c. maple syrup     2 tsp. baking powder
1 egg     1 tsp. salt

Cream butter; add the syrup and egg. Sift in dry ingredients and mix well. Drop by teaspoonfuls onto buttered baking sheets with plenty of room between. Bake at 400°F until golden.

## ❦ Chewy Drop Cookies

½ c. unsalted butter, softened
1 c. sugar
2 eggs, stiffly beaten
1 tsp. milk
2 tsp. baking powder
pinch salt
1 c. flour

Cream butter and sugar, then add eggs and milk. Sift in baking powder, salt, and flour and mix well. Drop by teaspoonfuls onto buttered baking sheets with plenty of room between. Bake at 400°F for just a few minutes, watching closely to prevent scorching.

*Variation:*
Orange Drop Cookies: To the above add 1 tsp. grated orange rind and ⅛ tsp. baking soda, and substitute 1 tsp. vanilla for milk.

## ❦ Sponge Drops

*Adapted from* Recipes Tried and True by Cooks

3 eggs, beaten light
¾ c. sugar
1 c. flour
⅓ tsp. salt
1 tsp. baking powder

To the eggs add sugar and mix well. Sift in remaining ingredients, then drop by teaspoonfuls onto buttered baking sheets. Bake at 400°F till lightly golden.

## ❦ Brown Sugar Drops

*A very plain cookie.*

1 c. brown sugar, firmly packed
1 large egg
¾ tsp. baking powder
¼ tsp. baking soda dissolved
   in ¼ c. buttermilk

½ c. unsalted butter
1½ c. flour
¼ tsp. salt
1 tsp. almond extract

Cream sugar with butter; add egg. Sift in dry ingredients, then add buttermilk mixture and extract. Drop on buttered baking sheets and bake 8–10 minutes at 325°F until lightly browned at edges.

*Variations:*

Brown Sugar Nut Drops (for the sweet tooth in your family): Add 1 c. chopped walnuts to batter. When cool, ice with:

| | |
|---|---|
| ½ c. unsalted butter, melted till light brown | 3 c. confectioner's sugar ¼ c. boiling water |

Melt butter in a saucepan over low flame. Add sugar and water, stirring to remove lumps. Remove from heat and whisk until thick and smooth. Spread over cookies.

Applesauce Drops: Add 1 c. applesauce and 1 tsp. cinnamon, omitting extract; increase flour to 2¼ c., baking soda to ½ tsp., and baking powder to 1 tsp. Ice as above.

Banana Drops: Add ½ c. ripe banana; increase flour to 2 c. and baking powder to 1 tsp.; decrease sugar to ¾ c., unless you like a very sweet cookie. Omit extract and sprinkle cinnamon and sugar over cookies before baking. Do not ice, and take care not to scorch.

*A Smart Table-Top Model*

# Ginger Drops I

| | |
|---|---|
| 1 c. sugar | 2 c. molasses |
| 1 c. sour cream | 1⅓ c. unsalted butter |
| 4 tsp. baking soda | 2 tsp. ground ginger |
| 1 tsp. cinnamon | 4 eggs |

flour to make a soft dough—about 5 c.

Mix all together well and drop onto buttered baking sheets. Bake at 350°F till done. Watch closely to prevent burning.

### Variation:

For New Year's Eve Clock Cookies: Make above ginger cookies large. Decorate with a clock face made of an icing of powdered sugar and heavy cream mixed together until smooth; apply with a toothpick twelve dashes around the edge of the cookie, and two hands pointed near the hour of 12:00.

■■■■■■■■■■■■■■■■■■■■■■■■■■■■■■■■■■■■■■■■■■

# Ginger Drops II

*Reader testers in Illinois and Pennsylvania said: "Simply delighted with these cookies" and "Especially like these cookies because they are easy to make and not too sweet."*—The Farmer's Wife Magazine

| | |
|---|---|
| 1 c. unsalted butter, softened | 1 c. sugar |
| 2 eggs | 1 c. molasses |
| 1 tbsp. baking soda dissolved in 1 c. warm water | 5 c. flour |
| | 1 tbsp. ground ginger |
| 1 tsp. salt | 1 c. raisins |

Cream butter and sugar. Beat well, then add eggs one at a time, beating thoroughly after each addition. Add molasses and mix well. Add baking soda mixture alternately with dry ingredients sifted together. Mix in raisins and drop by teaspoonfuls onto buttered baking sheets, leaving plenty of space between. Bake at 375°F for about 15 minutes.
*(A Pillsbury flour recipe).*

---

# ❦ Welsh Currant Cakes

*Adapted from* The United States Regional Cook Book

2 c. unsalted butter, softened
2¼ c. sugar
6 eggs
3 c. flour
1 tsp. nutmeg
¼ tsp. salt
1½ c. currants tossed with a little flour
(or substitute chopped raisins)

Cream butter and sugar, then add eggs one at a time. Beat well. Slowly sift in flour, nutmeg, and salt. Add currants. Mix and drop by teaspoonfuls onto well-buttered baking sheets. Bake at 375°F for about 10 minutes, until lightly browned.

## ❦ Walnut Cookies

1 tsp. baking soda dissolved in 1 c. buttermilk
6 c. flour
3 eggs
2 c. sugar
½ c. walnuts, chopped

Mix, adding walnuts last, then drop onto buttered baking sheets and bake at 350°F till just done.

- - - - - - - - - - - - - - - - - - - - - - - - - - - - - - - - - - - - - -

*Following are three "butterball"-style cookies, adapted from* **Favorite Recipes of the King's Daughters and Sons.** *Photos of such confections appear in* **The Farmer's Wife** *from time to time, without instruction.*

## ❦ Molasses Butterballs

1 c. unsalted butter, softened
¼ c. molasses
2 c. flour
½ tsp. salt
2 c. walnuts, chopped
confectioner's sugar for rolling

Cream butter; add molasses. Sift in flour and salt, then mix in nuts. Form into 1-inch balls and place on unbuttered baking sheets. Bake at 350°F for about 25 minutes, until lightly browned. Remove from sheets and roll in confectioner's sugar.

# ❦ Almond Butterballs

1 c. unsalted butter, softened
¼ c. confectioner's sugar
1 tsp. almond extract
2 c. flour
1 c. blanched almonds, chopped

Cream butter and sugar, add extract, then sift in flour. Mix in almonds. Form into 1-inch balls and place on unbuttered baking sheets. Bake at 350°F for about 20 minutes.

# ❦ Date Butterballs

½ c. unsalted butter, softened
⅓ c. confectioner's sugar
1 tbsp. milk
1 tsp. vanilla
1¼ c. flour
¼ tsp. salt
1 c. dates, pitted and finely chopped
½ c. walnuts, finely chopped
confectioner's sugar for rolling

Cream butter and sugar. Mix in milk and vanilla, then sift in flour and salt. Finally, stir in dates and nuts and mix well. Form into 1-inch balls and place on unbuttered baking sheets. Bake at 350°F for about 20 minutes, until lightly browned. Remove from sheets and roll in confectioner's sugar.

# ❦ Boston Drops

½ c. unsalted butter,
softened
¾ c. sugar
1 egg
1½ c. flour
½ tsp. baking powder
¼ tsp. salt
1 tsp. cinnamon
½ c. chopped raisins
¼ c. walnuts, chopped

Cream butter and add sugar slowly, creaming them together. Add egg, then sift in 1 c. flour, baking powder, salt, and cinnamon. Sift remainder of flour into raisins and nuts, mix, and add to batter. Mix thoroughly and drop from teaspoon 1 inch apart on buttered baking sheets. Bake at 400°F for 10 to 15 minutes.

*Variations:*
Dutch Drops: Substitute ½ c. blanched chopped almonds for walnuts, and ½ tsp. lightly crushed anise seed for cinnamon. Omit raisins.

English Drops: Add ½ c. cold coffee; increase sugar to 1 c. and flour to 1¾ c. Omit raisins.

# ❦ Taffy Drops

*A sweet, chewy drop cookie, adapted from* The Pennsylvania Dutch
Cook Book.

⅓ c. unsalted butter, melted
¾ c. molasses, warmed
2 c. brown sugar
2 c. flour
½ tsp. baking soda dissolved in 1 tsp. hot water
1 c. unsweetened grated cocoanut

Beat together butter and molasses; gradually beat in sugar. Sift in flour.
Add baking soda and cocoanut and mix well. Refrigerate overnight.
Drop by teaspoonfuls onto buttered baking sheets, leaving plenty of
room between. Bake at 350°F for about 15 minutes.

### Variation:
Taffy Nut Drops: Add ½ c. chopped walnuts instead of cocoanut.

# Cocoanut Brownies

*Mrs. A. L. H., Illinois*

1 c. buttermilk
1 c. molasses
1 c. light brown sugar
1 egg
piece of unsalted butter size of an egg (about 4 tbsp.)
1 tsp. baking soda dissolved in 1 tbsp. milk
3⅓ c. flour
2 c. unsweetened grated cocoanut

Cream together first four ingredients, then cream in butter. Add baking soda mixture; sift in flour and mix in cocoanut. Drop from a teaspoon onto buttered baking sheets a little way apart. Bake at 350°F until lightly golden.

*Variation:*
One can use raisins instead of cocoanut.

# ❦ Chocolate Drops

1 egg, well beaten
1 c. brown sugar
½ c. unsalted butter, softened
2 squares Baker's bittersweet chocolate, melted
1½ c. flour, or mix equal parts white and wheat flour
¼ tsp. salt
2 tsp. baking soda
1½ tsp. baking powder
½ c. buttermilk
½ tsp. vanilla

Combine egg, sugar, butter, and chocolate. Beat well. Sift in dry ingredients. Add liquids and nuts. Mix thoroughly. Drop from a teaspoon onto buttered baking sheets about an inch apart. Bake at 350°F for about 15 minutes.

*Variation:*
Chocolate Nut Drops: Add ½ c. chopped walnuts to the batter.

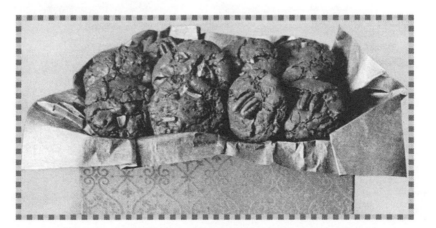

# APPROVED! A VISIT TO THE HOME OF A TYPICAL READER TESTER—MRS. HARRY A. HASS OF GREEN ACRES

*May 1937*

If you ever baked cookies for boys you will know that this picture shows a real "consumer" test. For David and Kendall Hass, Wisconsin farm boys, are just like all other boys in the world when it comes to eating cookies (and raw cookie dough, too, for that matter). When you get boys like these in the same kitchen with cookies only one thing can happen.

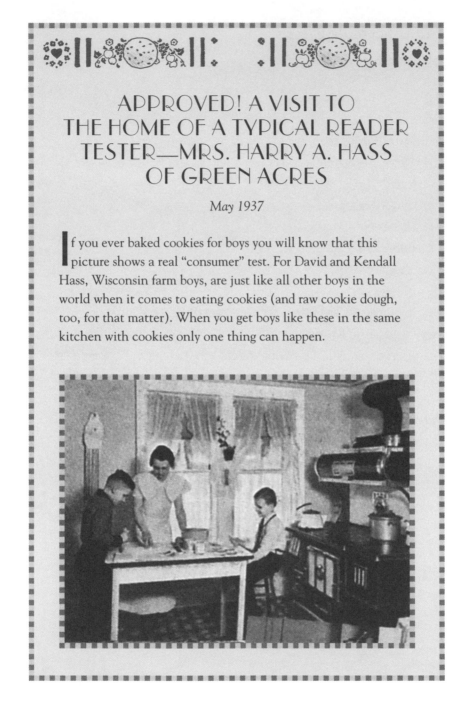

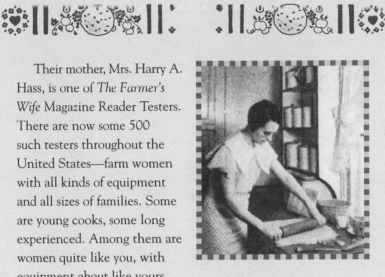

Their mother, Mrs. Harry A. Hass, is one of *The Farmer's Wife* Magazine Reader Testers. There are now some 500 such testers throughout the United States—farm women with all kinds of equipment and all sizes of families. Some are young cooks, some long experienced. Among them are women quite like you, with equipment about like yours.

It happens that Mrs. Hass was one of 100 Reader Testers who recently tried a certain brand of flour. They not only noted how the flour performed under their particular home conditions, and what kind of products it made, but they checked up on the manufacturer's recipes to see whether they were of the right size for farm families and whether they were easy to follow. The women's families, who ate the finished products, were the members of the "jury" when it came to taste.

Judging by the looks on the Hass boys' faces, the cookies were an entire success.

# ❦ Iced Chocolate Drops

½ c. unsalted butter, softened
1 c. light brown sugar
1 egg
¼ tsp. baking soda
2 tsp. baking powder
1½ c. flour
½ c. buttermilk
2 squares bittersweet Baker's chocolate, melted

Cream butter and sugar; add egg and beat well. Sift baking soda and baking powder with the flour and add alternately with buttermilk. Add the chocolate (and nuts if desired). Drop on buttered baking sheets and bake at 350°F until done. Ice with:

1 egg
2 c. powdered sugar
1 tsp. butter, melted
1 square bittersweet Baker's chocolate, melted

Beat the egg slightly and add the sugar, beating until smooth. Add the butter and chocolate and spread on the cookies. If frosting is a bit stiff, add cream to make it the right consistency to spread.

*Variation:*
Chocolate Nut Drops: Add 1 c. chopped nuts to the batter.

# ❦ Mincemeat Goodies

*Mrs. L. M. S., Minnesota*

1 c. unsalted butter, softened

2 c. sugar

3 eggs, well beaten

1 c. mincemeat

1 tbsp. baking soda dissolved in 2 tbsp. hot water

2 to 3 c. flour

⅛ tsp. ground ginger

1 tsp. each ground cloves, cinnamon, and nutmeg

½ c. walnuts, chopped and dredged in a little flour

Cream butter and sugar. Add eggs, then mincemeat, baking soda, and water; beat again. Combine 2 c. flour with spices and sift into the mixture before adding the nuts. Sift in more flour if not stiff enough to drop from spoon on unbuttered baking sheets, or roll and cut with cutters. Bake at 350°F till done.

# ❦ Sour Cream Drop Cookies

*Light, puffy cookies. Be sure not to let these brown, since they will dry out quickly in the oven.*

| | |
|---|---|
| ¼ c. unsalted butter, softened | 1 tsp. baking powder |
| 1¾ c. sugar | ½ tsp. salt |
| 2 eggs, beaten | 1 tbsp. grated lemon rind |
| 1 c. sour cream | raisins for garnishing |
| 3 c. flour | granulated sugar for dusting |
| ½ tsp. baking soda | |

Cream butter and ½ c. sugar in a large bowl. Beat eggs with remaining sugar and sour cream and add to first mixture. Sift flour with baking soda, baking powder, and salt. Add lemon rind, then combine with rest of ingredients. Drop *small* spoonfuls onto buttered baking sheets. Top each cookie with 1 raisin and sprinkle with sugar. Bake at 400°F for 5 to 6 minutes, till very slightly browned at the edges. Remove at once to cooling racks.

### Variations—two ways with cinnamon:

Cinnamon Sour Cream Cookies: Add 1 tsp. vanilla and omit lemon rind and raisins; dust with ¼ c. sugar mixed with 2 tsp. cinnamon before baking.

Sour Cream Date Cookies: Substitute 2 c. brown sugar for white sugar, and 1 tsp. cinnamon and ¼ tsp. nutmeg for lemon rind. Add 2 c. chopped dates and 1 c. finely chopped walnuts. Omit raisins.

# USES FOR SOUR CREAM

by Virginia Carter Lee
*August 1916*

In almost any of the receipts in which whipped sweet cream is gently combined with the mixture, whipped sour cream may be substituted, provided a tiny pinch of baking soda is added with a little more sugar and flavoring extract.

Photo credit: James Blinn / Shutterstock

# ❦ Fruit Drops

| | |
|---|---|
| 1 c. unsalted butter, softened | 2 c. raisins, chopped |
| 3 c. brown sugar | 2 c. dried currants |
| 4 tbsp. milk | 1 c. walnuts, chopped |
| 4 eggs, lightly beaten | 1 tsp. cinnamon |
| 2 tsp. baking soda | 4 tsp. cream of tartar |
| 5 c. flour | |

Cream butter and sugar; add milk and eggs. Sift baking soda and half the flour together and add to the mixture. Add fruit and nuts and work well together, then add cinnamon. To the remainder of the flour add the cream of tartar and sift, then add to the dough. Drop by teaspoonfuls on buttered baking sheets some distance apart and bake at 400°F till done. These are delicious and will keep a long time.

# ❧ Delicious Drop Cookies

¾ c. unsalted butter, softened
1½ c. brown sugar
3 eggs, beaten
2½ c. flour
pinch salt
1½ c. dates, chopped

1 c. peanuts, skinned and chopped
½ tsp. each cinnamon,
    allspice, and ground cloves
1 tsp. baking soda dissolved
    in ½ c. hot water

Cream butter and sugar, then add eggs, flour, and salt. Mix and add remaining ingredients. Mix well and drop by small spoonfuls onto hot buttered baking sheets. Bake at 400°F till done.

# ❧ Honey Drop Hermits

1⅓ c. honey
½ c. unsalted butter
1 tsp. cinnamon
½ tsp. cloves
½ tsp. nutmeg

1 egg, beaten
3 to 3½ c. flour
½ tsp. salt
¾ tsp. baking soda dissolved in ¼ c. water
1 c. chopped raisins or ½ c. each nuts
    and raisins

Heat honey and butter together. Add spices to the mixture while it is hot. Cool and add egg. Alternately add flour and salt, sifted together, and baking soda in water, then raisins (and nuts if desired). Beat well. Drop on greased pans and bake at 375°F until just brown.

# ❦ Mrs. Sudduth's Cookies

*These cookies are delicious and when baked are very light.*
—The Farmer's Wife Magazine

1 c. sugar

½ c. unsalted butter, softened

1 c. cream (sour cream may be used, but if so use a small pinch of
   baking soda)

2 eggs

2 tsp. baking powder

2 tsp. vanilla

½ tsp. lemon extract

1½ to 2 c. flour, to make a very soft dough

Mix well. Drop onto buttered cookie sheets and bake at 350°F till done.

# ❧ Peanut Drop Cookies

½ c. unsalted butter, softened
½ c. smooth peanut butter
1 c. brown sugar
1 egg
½ tsp. salt
1⅔ c. flour

1 tsp. baking powder
½ tsp. baking soda
½ c. milk
1 c. salted peanuts, skinned and
   chopped

Cream butter and peanut butter; add sugar and cream until fluffy. Add egg, beat thoroughly, then add sifted dry ingredients alternately with milk. Divide dough in half; to one half add half of the chopped peanuts. Drop by small spoonfuls on greased tin, pressing lightly with a finger. Drop out the other half of the dough in small spoonfuls, stamp down with a glass covered with a damp cloth, and sprinkle with remaining peanuts. Bake at 375°F for 8 to 12 minutes. This recipe makes 60 cookies. If brown-coated salted nuts are used, put in a salt sack and rub to remove husks. Fan out husks by pouring from one pan to another in the wind.

**Variations:**

Walnut Drops: Substitute 1 c. chopped walnuts for peanuts and add 1 tsp. vanilla.

Hickory Nut Drops: Same as for Walnut Drops, substituting chopped hickory nuts for walnuts.

Currant Drops: Substitute 1½ c. currants for nuts, dredging them in a little flour before adding to the batter; increase sugar to 1¼ c. and add 1 tsp. vanilla.

# ❧ Eggless Cookies

*Grace I. Henderson*

*For those days when you must bake and there is very little in the larder. They are vastly improved by a generous sprinkling of granulated sugar just before baking; if you happen to have extract on hand, 1 tsp. mixed into the batter is a nice addition.*

| | |
|---|---|
| 1 c. sugar | ½ c. milk |
| ½ c. unsalted butter, | ½ tsp. baking soda |
|    softened or shortening | flour—about 3 c. |

Cream sugar with butter, then add remaining ingredients. Roll into small balls and place on unbuttered baking sheets, pressing down lightly with your fingers. Bake at 400°F. until puffy and lightly browned around the edges—about 8–10 minutes. This recipe will be found convenient when cream and eggs are scarce. They will keep nice and tender for weeks.

## ❦ Walnut Lace Cookies

*Adapted from* Favorite Recipes of the King's Daughters and Sons

| | |
|---|---|
| 2 tbsp. unsalted butter, softened | 4 tbsp. flour |
| 1½ c. brown sugar | ¼ tsp. baking powder |
| 1 egg, beaten | 1½ c. walnuts, very finely chopped |

Cream butter and sugar, then add egg. Sift flour and baking powder into nuts, then stir into butter mixture. Drop by teaspoonfuls onto very well buttered baking sheets, with plenty of room between. Bake at 375°F for about 7 minutes, taking care not to scorch because the walnuts will take on an unpleasant flavor. Cool before removing to racks.

## ❦ Rich Peanut Butter Cookies

*Another variation on peanut cookies, this one not dropped, exactly, but formed into balls and flattened with a fork.*

| | |
|---|---|
| 1 c. unsalted butter, softened | 3 c. flour |
| 1 c. white sugar | 1 tsp. baking soda |
| 1 c. brown sugar | ½ tsp. salt |
| 1 c. peanut butter | 1 tsp. vanilla |
| 2 eggs, beaten | |

Cream butter and sugars, then add peanut butter and mix well. Add eggs, then dry ingredients, sifted together, and vanilla. Mix well and shape into balls. Place about 2 inches apart on sheet and press two ways with a fork to flatten and mark. Bake in a moderate oven (375°F) until delicately browned.

## ❦ Bran Drop Cookies

*Mrs. D. D., Ohio*

¼ c. unsalted butter, softened
½ c. sugar
1 egg
½ c. raisins, or ¼ c. raisins
   and ¼ c. nuts
1 c. bran

¾ c. flour
1 tsp. baking powder
¼ tsp. salt
½ tsp. cinnamon
¼ tsp. ground cloves

Cream butter; add sugar and egg. Mix in raisins (and nuts if desired), then bran, then the remaining dry ingredients sifted together three times. Bake at 400°F for about 20 minutes.

## ❦ Bread Crumb Cookies

*Mrs. C. H., North Dakota*

1 c. breadcrumbs
1 c. sugar
1 c. cream
½ c. unsalted butter, softened
1 egg

1 tsp. vanilla
2 c. flour
½ tsp. cinnamon
½ tsp. cloves
½ c. raisins

Mix first six ingredients together, sift in flour and spices, then work in raisins. Drop by teaspoonfuls onto buttered baking sheets and bake at 350°F until done, 8–12 minutes.

## ❧ Goober Cookies

1½ c. cornmeal
1½ c. finely ground peanuts
    (peanut flour)
1 tsp. salt
2 tsp. baking powder
¾ c. corn syrup
1 c. raisins, chopped
2 eggs

Mix ingredients together. Drop onto buttered baking sheets and bake at 350°F until lightly browned.

## ❧ Corn Rookies

1 c. cornmeal
2 c. peanut butter
2 tsp. salt
1 c. raisins, chopped

Place the cornmeal in a shallow pan and heat in the oven at 350°F till lightly browned, stirring frequently. Heat the peanut butter in a pan over low heat on top of the stove; when hot, stir in cornmeal. Beat thoroughly and add raisins. Drop by teaspoonfuls onto buttered baking sheets and bake at 350°F till done.

# ❦ Traveler's Cookies

*Adapted from* Recipes Tried and True by Cooks

½ c. unsalted butter, softened

1 c. brown sugar

½ tsp. salt

2 tbsp. orange rind, grated

2 eggs

2 c. flour

1 tsp. baking powder

¼ tsp. baking soda

½ c. walnuts, chopped

8 oz. bittersweet chocolate, roughly chopped

Cream butter and sugar; add salt and orange rind. Beat in eggs one at a time, sift in flour, baking powder, and baking soda, then mix in nuts and chocolate. Drop by teaspoonfuls onto buttered baking sheets and bake at 375°F for 10–12 minutes.

# ❧ Dainties

*Adapted from* Hot Recipes

⅔ c. unsalted butter, softened
1½ c. confectioner's sugar
2 eggs, separated
1 tsp. vanilla
2 c. flour
½ tsp. salt
jam for filling

Cream butter and 1 c. sugar, then add egg yolks and vanilla. Sift in flour and salt and mix well. Drop by teaspoonfuls onto unbuttered baking sheets. Make thumbprints in each cookie and fill with ¼ tsp. jam. Beat egg whites with a pinch of salt and add remaining ½ c. sugar. Beat until stiff. Top each cookie with a bit of meringue and bake at 300°F for about 30 minutes.

## Oatmeal Cookies

### ❦ Oatmeal Cookies I

1½ c. unsalted butter, softened
1½ c. sugar
2 eggs
2 tsp. baking powder
1 tsp. ground cinnamon
2 c. flour
⅓ c. milk or water
2 c. rolled oats

Cream butter and sugar, then add eggs. Sift in baking powder, cinnamon, and flour, then add liquid and, finally, oats. Mix well and drop on buttered baking sheets. Bake at 350°F until browned around edges.

# ❧ Oatmeal Cookies II
*E. A., Indiana*

1 c. unsalted butter
2 c. rolled oats
2 c. brown sugar
2 eggs
1 tsp. baking soda dissolved in 1 c. buttermilk
3 c. flour
1 tsp. vanilla
½ c. nuts, if desired

Melt butter and mix with oats. Add eggs to sugar and combine thoroughly, then add oatmeal mixture. Add buttermilk mixture alternately with flour, then mix in vanilla and nuts, if desired. Drop by teaspoonfuls on buttered baking sheets and bake at 350°F for about 10 minutes.

### *Variation:*
Oatmeal Maple Cookies: Substitute 1 c. maple syrup for brown sugar, ¼ c. plain milk for buttermilk, 1 tsp. baking powder for baking soda.

# ❧ Oatmeal Cookies III

*This time, with nuts, raisins, and a dash of molasses.*

¾ c. unsalted butter, softened
1 c. sugar
1 egg
2½ c. rolled oats
2½ c. flour
4 tsp. baking powder
1 tsp. cinnamon
½ tsp. salt
1 tbsp. molasses
¾ c. cold water, approximately
½ c. raisins and walnuts, chopped

Cream butter with sugar, add egg, then mix in remaining ingredients, using enough water to form a drop batter. Add raisins and nuts last. Mix well and drop by teaspoonfuls onto buttered baking sheets. Bake at 350°F until lightly browned around edges.

# ❦ Oatmeal Lace Cookies

*A crisp and nearly flourless cookie held together by caramelized sugar. This one is adapted from* Cohasset Entertains.

1 c. unsalted butter
2½ c. light brown sugar
2¼ c. rolled oats
1 tbsp. flour
1 egg, beaten
1 tsp. vanilla

Melt butter over low flame. Add sugar and stir until dissolved. Remove from heat and stir in oats and flour. Let stand 5 minutes, then add egg and vanilla. Drop by teaspoonfuls onto well-buttered baking sheets, leaving plenty of room between. Bake at 375°F for 5–7 minutes, until lightly browned at the edges; check often to prevent scorching. Cool on sheets before removing to rack.

*Variation:*
*A slightly chewy, less sweet version of the original. Delicious!*

Cocoanut Lace Cookies: Substitute 1 c. shredded unsweetened cocoanut for 1 c. of the oats, and ½ c. honey for ½ c. of the brown sugar. Drop onto well-buttered baking sheets and press lightly with fingers to flatten cookies to the size of silver-dollar coins. Cooking time is slightly less than for Oatmeal Lace Cookies.

# ❦ Chocolate Oatmeal Drops

*Chocolate chip cookies weren't invented till near the demise of* The Farmer's Wife. *Here's a version, adapted from* Hot Recipes, *that approximates a cookie that would have come out of the FW kitchen.*

1 c. unsalted butter, softened
½ c. sugar
1 c. brown sugar, packed
2 eggs
1 tsp. vanilla
1 c. flour
½ tsp. salt
1 tsp. baking soda
1 c. rolled oats
1 c. bittersweet chocolate, grated or chopped

Cream butter and sugars. Add eggs and vanilla and beat well. Sift in flour, salt, and baking soda and stir to mix. Add oats and chocolate, stir, and drop by spoonfuls onto buttered baking sheets. Bake at 375°F for 8–10 minutes.

HIS ONE WEAKNESS-
. . . Toll House Cookies from home. Now that Nestle's Semi-Sweet Chocolate is harder to get—because so much chocolate is needed for the armed forces for emergency and combat rations—put it to the best possible use. Make up a batch of those golden-brown, crunchy Toll House Cookies and send it to that soldier boy of yours. He always did go for those crisp, brown cookies containing whole pieces of Nestle's Semi-Sweet Chocolate. You'll find the easy-to-make recipe on every package.
When your dealer is temporarily out of Nestle's Chocolate products, please be patient. Remember the demands of our armed forces are heavy, but they must come first.
NESTLE'S
SEMI-SWEET CHOCOLATE
TOLL HOUSE COOKIES
SEMI-SWEET CHOCOLATE
BACK THE ATTACK WITH WAR BONDS

# Spiced Oatmeal Cookies

1 c. unsalted butter, softened
2 c. brown sugar
2 eggs
1 c. buttermilk
2½ c. flour
1 tsp. baking soda
¾ tsp. salt

3 tsp. mixed spice (taken from a
    mixture made from 4 tbsp.
    cinnamon, 2 tbsp. nutmeg,
    2 tbsp. ground allspice or cloves)
2 c. rolled oats
2 c. raisins

Cream butter and sugar. Beat eggs and mix with buttermilk. Sift flour with baking soda, salt, and spices, and then mix with the rolled oats and raisins. Add liquid and dry ingredients alternately to the creamed mixture. Drop on buttered baking sheets and bake at 375°F for about 15 minutes.

*Variations:*
Use 3 c. whole-wheat flour instead of white flour.
Use a scant cup of sweet milk instead of buttermilk; substitute ½ tsp. baking powder for baking soda.
Grind rolled oats and raisins in the blender to get a fine texture.
Substitute bran for oats to create a bran drop cookie. *Note: Oat bran flour can be purchased at health and kitchen specialty stores, and some supermarkets.*

Pumpkin Drops: Add 1 c. pumpkin puree, ½ c. shredded unsweetened cocoanut, and ½ c. walnuts. Substitute ¾ c. regular milk for buttermilk, and 1 tsp. baking powder for baking soda.

Cocoanut Oatmeal Cookies: Add 1 c. shredded unsweetened cocoanut.

# ❦ Ranch Cookies

*Adapted from* Recipes from Maa Eway

¼ c. unsalted butter, softened
½ c. brown sugar
½ c. white sugar
1 egg
½ c. flour
¼ tsp. baking powder
½ tsp. baking soda
1 c. rolled oats
½ c. grated unsweetened cocoanut
½ c. pecans, chopped

Cream butter with sugars and add egg. Sift in flour, baking powder, and baking soda. Mix in remaining ingredients and drop by teaspoonfuls on buttered baking sheets. Flatten with fingers. Bake at 350°F for 10–15 minutes.

# Macaroons

## ❦ Cocoanut Cornflake Macaroons

2 egg whites
1 c. sugar
1 c. unsweetened shredded
   cocoanut

1 tbsp. flour
½ c. chopped pecans
2 c. crisp cornflakes
1 tsp. vanilla

Beat egg whites till very stiff; gradually beat in sugar until thick and gluey. Gently fold in cocoanut, flour, nuts, cornflakes, and vanilla. Drop by spoonfuls onto buttered parchment paper–lined baking sheets. Bake at 325°F until lightly golden.

# ❦ Wartime Oatmeal Macaroons

*A resourceful* Farmer's Wife *wartime recipe, compensating for a scarcity of sugar.*

1 tbsp. unsalted butter, melted and cooled
1 egg
½ c. corn syrup
2 c. rolled oats
½ tsp. salt
1 tsp. baking powder

Add egg to butter and beat well, then add corn syrup. Add remaining ingredients and mix. Drop by spoonfuls onto buttered baking sheets and bake at 350°F for about 15 minutes.

# ❦ Almond Macaroons

*A very delicate, delicious cookie. Recipes nearly identical to this one were the stand-bys in England until the twentieth century, when ingredients other than almonds found their way into the mix, according to the late English food writer and historian Alan Davidson. Cream of tartar will assist in stiffening the egg whites but is not necessary, if you are patient, and adding it will result in an airier cookie.*

2 egg whites
⅛ tsp. cream of tartar (optional)
1½ c. confectioner's sugar, sifted
½ c. almond flour, pressed through a sieve if grind is not very fine

Beat egg whites till very stiff, with cream of tartar if desired. Very gradually incorporate sugar till the mixture is thick and gluey. Fold in almond flour and drop (or pipe) onto buttered parchment paper–lined baking sheets. Bake at 325°F for 10–15 minutes, until just set—do not allow to brown. Remove immediately from paper.

### Variations:

Hickory Nut Macaroons: Substitute 1 c. hickory nuts, ground fine in food processor then sieved, for almond flour.

Pistachio Macaroons: Same as above, substituting 1 c. pistachios for hickory nuts.

Cocoanut Macaroons: Substitute 1 c. cocoanut for nuts.

Fruit Macaroons: Sprinkle up to ½ c. currants or very finely chopped dates or raisins over batter just before spooning onto baking sheets.

Chocolate Macaroons: *This (quite toothsome) variation must have appealed to the farmer's wife's sense of thrift; don't throw away those egg yolks—find another use for them!* To beaten egg whites, fold in two slightly beaten egg yolks. Mix almond flour with ½ c. grated semi-sweet chocolate (or run ½ c. chocolate chips through the blender, till pulverized) and a few drops of vanilla. Bake 12–15 minutes. This will result in a delicate version of a chocolate chip cookie. Alternately: Melt ½ c. semi-sweet chocolate and allow to cool completely. Mix into egg yolks and fold in.

# ❦ Oatmeal Macaroons

*A decidedly odd-ball variety.*

| | |
|---|---|
| ¼ c. rolled oats | 1 c. confectioner's sugar, sifted |
| 1 egg, beaten | 1 tbsp. unsalted butter, melted |
| 2 tbsp. cream | dash of cinnamon |
| 2 tbsp. milk | 2 tsp. baking powder |
| 2 tbsp. water | 1 c. flour |

Put oats in a large bowl and cover with egg, cream, milk, and water. Let stand until the oats have soaked up all the moisture, then add sugar, butter, and cinnamon. Sift baking powder and flour together and add to the mixture, adding more flour if necessary to make a stiff dough. Shape into balls as large as walnuts and bake in a moderate oven (about 325°F) until just done.

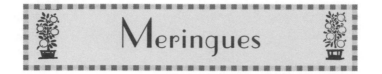

# Meringues

## WHEN EGGS ARE PLENTIFUL

*March 1928*

Meringues furnish a delightful way of providing dainty egg dishes, almost fairy-like in their texture and lightness.

A meringue is sweetened white of egg cooked over hot liquid or baked. The usual way of cooking over hot liquid is to complete a cooked custard and then dot the beaten whites on tablespoonfuls over the top while hot. The heat of the liquid will set the egg white enough so that it will hold its shape.

Meringues are more often baked, however. The secret of making excellent meringues lies in beating the eggs exactly right and in the baking. Sugar helps the egg to hold air and

remain stiff without getting dry. If the sugar is added gradually while beating, the whipped egg is smooth, light and silvery white in color. Too much sugar makes the meringue flatten out when spread over the baking board.

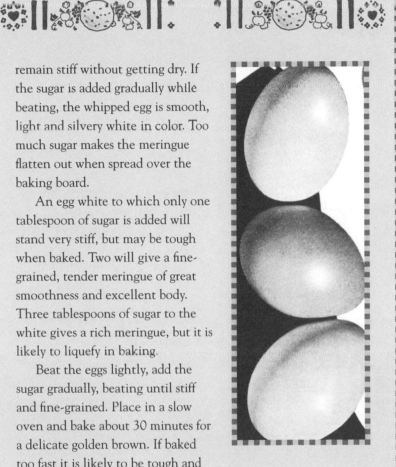

An egg white to which only one tablespoon of sugar is added will stand very stiff, but may be tough when baked. Two will give a fine-grained, tender meringue of great smoothness and excellent body. Three tablespoons of sugar to the white gives a rich meringue, but it is likely to liquefy in baking.

Beat the eggs lightly, add the sugar gradually, beating until stiff and fine-grained. Place in a slow oven and bake about 30 minutes for a delicate golden brown. If baked too fast it is likely to be tough and watery, and to fall as soon as it is taken from the oven. A meringue is best when finished just before serving.

## ❦ Simplest Meringue

2 egg whites, beaten stiff
½ c. confectioner's sugar
½ tsp. vanilla

Fold sugar and vanilla into egg whites. Drop in small shapes on buttered waxed paper. Ten or twelve may be made from one white. Bake *very* slowly (*dry* rather than *bake*) at about 225°F for about half an hour or longer.

Variations of the foregoing: Sprinkle with dessicated cocoanut before baking. Add 2 tsp. cocoa powder with the sugar. Finely chopped nuts may be sprinkled over before baking. Tiny candies, such as sugared caraway seeds, may be put on top before baking. After baking, two may be put together, back to back, with any frosting (or jam).

# ❧ Meringue (Foundation Recipe)

| | |
|---|---|
| 3 large egg whites, | 1 c. sugar |
|    at room temperature | 1 tsp. vinegar |
| ¼ tsp. salt | 1 tsp. water |
| ¼ tsp. cream of tartar | 1 tsp. vanilla |

Add salt and cream of tartar to egg whites and beat to a stiff but
not dry foam. Add sugar by tablespoons at first, alternately with the
liquids mixed together, then beat in the rest of the sugar until it is well
blended and the mixture has good piling quality.

For Individual Meringues: Shape as "nests" for individual servings on a
baking sheet covered with buttered waxed or parchment paper. Bake
about 1 hour at 225°F. Loosen from paper before they are cool. Fill
as desired, with whipped cream and fruit, or fruit-flavored ice cream
garnished with a few choice pieces of fruit.

For Meringue Kisses: To one half of the above meringue recipe add
½ c. mixed candied fruit and ½ c. chopped nuts. To the other half
add ½ c. crushed cornflakes and ½ c. shredded cocoanut. Drop by
teaspoonfuls on buttered plain brown paper on a baking sheet and
bake at 250°F about 45 minutes.

For Meringue Kisses another way: Add 1 c. each chopped dates
and walnuts.

For Brown Sugar Meringues: Substitute ½ c. light brown sugar for ½ c.
white in the original recipe. Bake at 225°F for about 1 hour. Serve with
plain, chocolate, or butterscotch ice cream and top with black walnut
or pecan nutmeats.

# ❧ Currant Meringues

*You may use jam for this recipe instead of fresh fruit, in which case the sugar should be reduced to ½ c.*

1 pint green currants, cooked
1 c. sugar
½ c. bread crumbs, sifted
2 eggs, separated
4 tbsp. butter

Cook 1 pint of green currants until soft, mash, and add 1 c. sugar, ½ c. sifted bread crumbs, the yolks of two eggs, and a piece of butter the size of an egg (4 tbsp.). Mix thoroughly and fold in whites of two eggs, beaten stiff. Drop onto buttered baking sheets and bake at 250°F for 1 hour. Allow to cool mostly on baking sheet before removing to racks. These odd, sweet confections would be put to good use crumbled on top of ice cream.

## Meringues Glacées

2 c. sugar
¾ c. water
5 egg whites
¼ tsp. salt
1 tsp. vanilla

Combine the water and sugar in a smooth saucepan and stir until the mixture boils, using a wooden spoon. Never stir after it boils, and have the flame so regulated that the syrup cooks evenly all over the pan. Cook until it reaches the soft-ball stage (234–240°F registered on a candy thermometer).

Let the syrup stand on the stove as you beat the egg whites to a stiff froth. Then add the syrup slowly to the eggs, beating until the meringue is cold. Stir in the vanilla. Drop on buttered waxed or parchment paper from a teaspoon for small cookies. Bake 1 hour in a slow oven (250°F). The above recipe makes 12 shells. They may also be shaped with a pastry bag and made into rounds the size of mushroom caps and into short upright pieces like mushroom stems. Put caps and stems together while hot. Or put together 2 shells with ice cream in between. Garnish with whipped cream and top with maraschino cherries.

# TABLE TALK FOR THE COUNTRY COOKIE JAR

Clara E. Wells

*October 1914*

As the "stolen fruits" from the cookie jar of our far off youth ever seemed "sweetest," I herewith pass on some of my favorite recipes, and those "begged, borrowed or stolen" from country gentlewomen who do not have to economize so rigidly in their land "flowing with milk and honey" as must the city housewife.

These favorites have been served to the past and present generation though they have never appeared in print.

As the nut and fruit cookies "ripen" with age, the recipes for them should be doubled and the extra supply of cookies be hidden away in the large cookie jar for later use.

*(More thorough recipes for most of these cookies appear elsewhere in this book. I include these here as they appear in the magazine, as a point of interest. How would you fare baking from these sparse directions?)*

**Hickorynut Cookies:** One cupful of chopped hickory nut meats, one cupful of sweet milk, two eggs, one cupful and a half of maple sugar, teaspoonful of baking powder sifted in two quarts of flour. Bake in a moderate oven and glaze with honey, pressing half a hickory nut meat in center of each cookie.

**Walnut Cookies:** Half cupful of walnuts meats, cupful of buttermilk, teaspoonful of soda, quart and half of flour, three eggs, two cupfuls of sugar.

**Chocolate Cookies:** One cupful of sweet cream, half cupful of butter, four eggs, two cups of sugar, teaspoonful of baking powder sifted in quart of flour. Bake in quick oven, glaze with sweetened chocolate or put half cake of sweetened melted chocolate in batter.

**Hermit Cookies:** One and a half cupfuls of sugar, two thirds cupful of sugar, three eggs, two tablespoons of Orleans molasses, one teaspoonful of soda. Beat soda in molasses. Two cupfuls of raisins, one teaspoonful of spices. Two quarts of flour.

**Cocoanut Cookies:** One cupful of sweetened cocoanut, whites of three eggs, one cupful of sugar, one cupful of sweet cream, teaspoonful of baking powder. Bake in quick oven, glaze with honey, and sprinkle with cocoanut.

**Caraway Cookies:** One cupful of sweet milk, one cupful of butter, one teaspoonful of baking powder, half cup of caraway seeds, two cupfuls of maple sugar, quart and half of flour. Roll thin and bake in quick oven.

**School Lunch Cookies:** One cupful of lard, one cupful of buttermilk, two cupfuls of sugar, one egg, teaspoonful of baking powder, two quarts of flour. Bake in quick oven, ice with pink sugar.

**Harvest Ginger Cookies:** One pint of Orleans molasses, cupful of lard or butter, cupful of sugar, cupful of buttermilk, teaspoonful of soda, two quarts of flour. Roll and bake in quick oven. They will disappear quickly when served as afternoon lunch in the harvest field.

Nearly every farmer's wife boils down a jug or more of cider for use in her mince pies yet ignores . . . another good use to which it can be put:

**Boiled Cider Cookies:** One cupful lard and one cupful sugar creamed together. Add one cupful boiled cider, one teaspoonful soda, and a taste of cloves and cinnamon. Beat one egg, adding a little salt, and then beat all together for five minutes. Add flour enough to make a moderately stiff dough and bake in moderate oven.

# Ice Box Cookies

Before there were Pillsbury slice-and-bake cookies for sale in the refrigerated section of the supermarket, there was the real-deal homemade variety. Ice box cookies are almost as easy to make as drop cookies, and they bake up into delicious, thin, crispy rounds. They enjoy one advantage over all other cookies: having rolled and stored them in the refrigerator (or freezer—up to three months!), the baker can simply slice off the number of cookies desired, place in the oven, and come back for more at a later time.

# SAY IT WITH COOKIES

*October 1920*

There's nothing quite like cookie-baking day. Nothing quite so cheerful in its floury confusion as the cookie-day kitchen, or so compelling as the spicy smell when each pan comes from the oven. Nothing quite so absorbing to the cook as this task which keeps both hands busy and demands a watchful eye on the oven and another on the children making inroads on the freshly baked heap.

There are ways to get around cutting out cookies, unless you want fancy shapes. Then a rich dough is rolled thin on canvas on board. But for plain, round cookies we learned one good method a few years ago—making the dough in a roll, then chilling and slicing it into thin rounds.

*Voila! Ice box cookies are born! Or as many of us call them these days, refrigerator cookies.*

# ❦ Ice Box Cookies

*Mrs. A. H. Burandt, manager of the Justamere Tea Room,*
*Brookings, South Dakota*

*This recipe—which makes enough for a party   was included in the*
*magazine on the occasion of the Farmer's Wife Master Farm Homemaker*
*dinner, an annual event that in 1931 was held at the State College of*
*Agriculture. Other offerings on that year's menu included a ginger ale salad*
*and a cranberry gelatin ring.*

1½ c. unsalted butter, melted
2 c. brown sugar
4 eggs, beaten light
5½ c. flour
1 tsp. soda
2 tsp. baking powder
1 c. chopped walnuts
½ tsp. mixed spice (see pg. 48)
1 tsp. salt

Mix together butter and sugar; add eggs. Combine the remaining
ingredients with the flour and add to the first mixture. Shape into logs,
wrap in waxed paper, and refrigerate overnight. Slice and place on
buttered baking sheets. Bake at 350°F until golden.

# Ice Box Cookies

*Just enough to fill the cookie jar.*

1½ c. unsalted butter, softened
1 c. sugar
1 c. brown sugar, firmly packed
3 eggs, slightly beaten
½ tsp. salt

1 tsp. cinnamon
½ tsp. baking soda
1 tsp. baking powder
4½ c. flour

Cream the butter and sugars. Add the eggs and beat well. Sift in salt, cinnamon, baking soda, baking powder, and flour; beat well. Shape into two logs, wrap in waxed paper, and refrigerate overnight. In the morning, slice, arrange on buttered baking sheets, and bake at 450°F until done.

### Variations:

Use 1¾ c. white sugar and omit brown. Omit spice.

For Lemon Cookies: Add ¼ tsp. lemon juice and 1 tsp. grated lemon rind.

For Orange Cookies: Add 2½ tsp. grated orange rind and ½ tsp. orange extract.

Divide dough into two parts. Add sliced dates to one part and unsweetened grated cocoanut to the other.

Add 1 tsp. vanilla to the dough and sprinkle cut cookies with sugar before baking.

Add ½ tsp. almond extract and 1 c. blanched chopped almonds.

# ❦ Chocolate Ice Box Cookies

*Kansas*

½ c. unsalted butter, softened
1 c. sugar
1 egg, beaten
2 squares bittersweet Baker's chocolate, melted
2 c. flour
¼ tsp. salt
2 tsp. baking powder
¼ c. milk

Cream the butter, add the sugar, and blend well. Add the egg and chocolate and beat. Add the sifted dry ingredients and milk alternately. Chill dough, and when firm, roll out and shape in logs the size of a tumbler. Chill again until firm, then cut into thin slices. Bake on buttered baking sheets at 350°F for about 10 minutes. If dough is put in refrigerator it may be kept several days wrapped in waxed paper.

# ❦ Butterscotch Ice Box Cookies

1½ c. unsalted butter, softened
2 c. brown sugar
2 eggs, well beaten
2 tsp. baking powder

3 c. flour, plus more as necessary to
form dough that can be shaped
into log

Cream butter; add sugar and eggs. Mix well. Add flour and baking powder sifted together. Mix to a dough (adding more flour as instructed above). Shape into logs, wrap in waxed paper, and chill or store in cool place, a refrigerator if available. Slice thin and bake on buttered and floured cookie sheet at 400°F until done.

*Variations:*
Butterscotch Cookies another way: Add 1 tsp. each vanilla, lemon, and orange extracts.

Cardamom Ice Box Cookies: Add 1 tbsp. ground cardamom seeds, ¼ tsp. salt, and a few drops heavy cream. Dust cut cookies with sugar before baking.

Honey Ice Box Cookies: Substitute ¾ c. honey and 1 c. white sugar for brown sugar, and 1 tsp. baking soda for 1 tsp. baking powder. Add ¼ tsp. almond extract and ½ tsp. salt.

Anise Ice Box Cookies: Substitute ½ c. confectioner's sugar for brown sugar. Add juice and grated rind of one lemon and 1 tbsp. anise seed.

Ginger Ice Box Cookies: Substitute ½ c. molasses and ½ c. white sugar for brown sugar, and 1 tsp. baking soda for 1 tsp. baking powder. Add 1 tsp. ground ginger, 2 tsp. finely chopped candied ginger, and ½ tsp. salt. *Check often during baking to prevent burning.*

# ❦ Apricot Oatmeal Cookies

1 c. unsalted butter, softened
¾ c. sugar
1 c. brown sugar, tightly packed
2 eggs
1 tsp. vanilla
1½ c. flour

1 tsp. salt
1 tsp. baking soda
3½ c. rolled oats
1½ c. dried apricots, finely chopped
1 c. pecans, chopped

Cream butter and sugars; add eggs and vanilla and mix well. Sift in flour, salt, and baking soda. Add remaining ingredients and mix well. Shape into 1-inch logs and wrap in waxed paper. Refrigerate overnight, then slice dough ½ inch thick and place on buttered baking sheets. Bake at 350°F for 10–15 minutes till lightly browned.

# CAN YOU JUGGLE RECIPES?

Greta Gray
*October 1920*

Variations in recipes according to the cupboard's contents are largely a matter of substitution. We women have had a recent experience in the use of substitutes for flour and sugar and we all learned a few new dishes, or some bread variations which we very much liked. We learned, for example, that if we have not enough wheat flour, we can use, instead of part of it, cold cooked cereal, corn meal, cornstarch, and other substitutes. If we have no pastry flour, we may use instead of it 2⅔ cups of bread flour and ⅓ cup of cornstarch. This gives better and more uniform results than do the average pastry flours.

Sometimes, when we make sugar-changes, we get into trouble with our results but this can be avoided. In using brown or powdered sugar for granulated sugar, use the same *weight* as for granulated sugar.

In place of 1 cup of sugar, we may use 1 cup of honey and 1–6 teaspoonful of soda (because honey is acid), 1⅓ c. molasses or

1⅔ c. syrup. The liquid called for in the recipe must be reduced by ¼ cup for each cup of honey, molasses or syrup used. Enough soda should be added to the molasses to neutralize its acidity and if baking powder is called for, the amount used should be reduced according to the measure of soda used.

Instead of syrup, use 1 cup sugar and ½ cup water boiled together flavored with maple or caramel. To prevent crystallization of the syrup, add ⅛ tsp. cream of tartar before boiling.

One egg white equals in leavening power 1 teaspoonful baking powder.

## ❧ Petticoat Tails

*Adapted from* Williamsburg Art of Cookery

*An icebox version of shortbread. Traditionally this would have been baked in a large round pan, scored into twelve even wedges with a central circle removed, to resemble an "outspread bell-hoop crinoline petticoat," according to Alan Davidson's* Penguin Companion to Food.

5 c. flour
1 c. confectioner's sugar

2 c. lightly salted butter, slightly softened

Sift flour and sugar together and cut in butter. Shape into logs, wrap in waxed paper, and refrigerate overnight. In the morning, slice thin and place on buttered baking sheets. Prick all over with a fork. Bake at 350°F until lightly golden.

Photo credit: Marie C. Fields/Shutterstock

# Rolled Cookies

Crisp and thin like ice box cookies but with one lovely feature: Rolled cookies can be cut out into any shape you desire. They can be tricky to work with, though. To minimize problems, roll out on a floured board (or one sprinkled with confectioner's sugar—this will keep the cookies from getting tough). Chill dough for an hour before rolling if it seems sticky. Or, roll between two layers of waxed paper. *The Farmer's Wife* would mostly have used a farm staple— butter—for these recipes. But some bakers prefer a mixture of half butter, half shortening or margarine, for less crumbly cookies.

# ❦ Sugar Cookies

The foundation rule for sugar cookies begins with the following:

½ c. fat
I c. sugar
I or 2 eggs

Milk is the next addition. If a very crispy cooky is desired, use only I tbsp. or omit altogether. For a softer cooky the amount of milk may reach ½ c., then add 2½ c. flour (more to roll out), 2 tsp. baking powder, ¼ to ½ tsp. salt (depending on amount of salt in fat used), and flavoring.

### To Mix the Dough:

Cream the fat; add sugar gradually, then the well-beaten eggs and the milk. Mix and sift dry ingredients and add to the first mixture. Remove a small portion, roll, and shape as desired. Chilling the dough in advance makes rolling it easier and requires less flour. It may be kept in a cool place overnight.... Much less flour is required if a floured cloth is used in place of the usual moulding board ... a heavy dishcloth is often used. Rub flour well into the meshes of the cloth. Do not bear down on the rolling pin but *lift it* as you roll, and use short, quick strokes. With good care such cloths need to be washed only occasionally.

Chocolate Cookies: Add ⅓ square melted Baker's chocolate to one-fourth of the mixture.

Raisin and Nut Cookies: Chop and add to the dough or sprinkle on top with sugar, before baking.

Cocoanut Cookies: Add ½ c. cocoanut to one-fourth the mixture.

Spice Cookies: Mix ½ tsp. cinnamon and ¼ tsp. each of ground cloves and nutmeg with another one-fourth of mixture, or sprinkle spices on top before cutting out.

Lemon or Orange Cookies: Flavor the dough with grated rind.

Sour Cream Sugar Cookies: Omit half the fat and half the baking powder. Add ½ c. sour cream and ¼ tsp. baking soda (sift with flour).

Sour Milk Sugar Cookies: Omit half the baking powder; add ½ c. sour milk (buttermilk may be substituted), ¼ tsp. soda, and ¼ c. fat to make them rich and soft.

## ❦ Good Cookies

2 c. sugar, plus extra for sprinkling
1 c. unsalted butter, softened
1 c. sour cream
3 eggs
1 tsp. baking soda
3 to 4 c. flour, to make a soft dough

Mix to a soft dough, roll thin on a floured board, cut out, and lay on buttered baking sheets. Sift granulated sugar over cookies and gently roll in. Bake at 400°F till just golden.

## ❧ Plain Cookies

1 c. sugar
½ c. plus 2 tsp. unsalted butter, softened
2 eggs
4 tbsp. heavy cream
2½ c. flour

Mix all together and roll out moderately thin. Cut with cutters and place on buttered baking sheets. Bake at 400°F till just golden. These are excellent.

## ❧ Crispy Sugar Cookies

1 c. unsalted butter, softened
2 c. sugar, plus extra for rolling
2 eggs, beaten
grated rind of 1 lemon
¼ c. heavy cream
4 c. flour
3 tsp. baking powder
½ tsp. nutmeg
1 tsp. salt

Cream butter and sugar, mixing till light. Add egg, lemon rind, and cream and beat well. Sift in dry ingredients a bit at a time, then roll out dough on a lightly floured board. Sprinkle liberally with sugar and roll over lightly. Cut with cutters and place on buttered baking sheets. Bake at 400°F for 8–10 minutes, until lightly brown.

# ❧ Good Sugar Cookies

*Ida L. Townsend*

½ c. unsalted butter, softened
1 c. sugar
2 eggs, well beaten
5 tbsp. sour cream
5 tbsp. buttermilk
pinch of salt

1 tsp. baking powder
½ tsp. baking soda
½ tsp. cinnamon
½ tsp. cloves
1½ to 2 c. flour, to make
a soft dough

Cream the butter and sugar together. Add the eggs, sour cream, and buttermilk, then the remaining ingredients sifted together. Mix well and roll out on a floured board. Cut and place on buttered baking sheets. Bake at 400°F till done.

■■■■■■■■■■■■■■■■■■■■■■■■■■■■■■■■■■■■■■■■■■■■■■■■

# ❧ Like the Ones Mother Used to Make

*Apparently, Mother knew what she was doing—no elaborate instructions for her!*

1 c. sour cream
½ c. unsalted butter, softened
1½ c. sugar
3 eggs
1 tsp. baking soda
sifted flour enough to roll

Mix, roll out, and bake at 350°F.

# ❦ Orange Sugar Cookies

1 c. unsalted butter, softened
1½ c. sugar
3 eggs
1 c. candied orange peel, finely chopped (see pg. 151)
2 tsp. baking powder
½ tsp. salt
4 to 5 c. flour
⅔ c. milk
1 tsp. orange extract

Cream butter; add sugar, eggs, orange
peel, and then sifted dry ingredients
alternately with milk and extract. Roll
and cut, or shape in balls and flatten
out. Place on buttered baking sheets
and bake at 400°F for 10 minutes.

## ❦ White Cookies

*Mrs. M. M. V., Montana*

| | |
|---|---|
| 1 c. unsalted butter, softened | 3 tbsp. milk |
| 3 c. flour | 1 tsp. baking soda |
| 2 eggs | ½ tsp. nutmeg |
| 1 c. sugar | |

Mix butter and flour as for pie crust. Break eggs into dish and mix with sugar, milk, baking soda, and nutmeg. Combine with flour mixture. Roll out, cut, and place on buttered baking sheets. Bake at 350°F till done.

---

## ❦ Vanilla Cookies

| | |
|---|---|
| 1½ c. sugar | 1 tbsp. milk |
| ½ c. unsalted butter, softened | 3¾ c. flour |
| 1 tsp. vanilla | ½ tsp. salt |
| 2 egg yolks | ½ tsp. baking soda |
| ½ c. sour cream | |

Cream sugar and butter, then add vanilla and egg yolks. Mix in sour cream and milk, then sift in flour, salt, and baking soda. Mix well to make a stiff dough. Cover and refrigerate 1 hour, then roll out very thin on a floured board and cut with cutters. Place on buttered baking sheets and bake at 375°F for about 10 minutes.

## ❦ Tea Cakes

*Following are dainty cakes for luncheon. "Flavor," if desired, with 1 tsp.*
*extract of your choice.*—The Farmer's Wife Magazine

1 c. sugar
½ c. unsalted butter, softened
⅓ c. milk
1 egg
flour to make a soft dough—up to 3 c.
½ tsp. extract of your choosing

Cream together the butter and sugar, then add remaining ingredients.
Flavor to taste with extract, roll, and cut in pieces 4 inches long,
1½ inches wide. Place on buttered baking sheets and bake at 350°F
till done.

# ❦ Valentine Cookies

Use your favorite cookie recipe, or any good recipe for sugar cookies
(see preceding recipes). Cut them with a heart-shaped cutter and
bake carefully. When cool, frost with a white frosting, and before the
frosting hardens, make a border all around the edge of each heart with
tiny little candies about the size of a small pea, which may be obtained
at any candy counter.

Heart-shaped cutters . . . may be made
by bending tin fruit or vegetable cans into
heart shapes of the size desired. Dainty little
cutters may be made from round cocoa
cans of the smallest size; half-pound baking
powder cans make a medium-size cutter,
while pound cans and the larger tin cans
in which canned fruits and vegetables are

purchased will make large heart shapes. Both ends of the can are
melted off, and by inserting an old knife the tin may be bent over the
edge of it to form the point of the heart. The top of the can may be
bent down, by the same means, to complete the heart shape.

*No doubt about it, sugar cookies were the mainstay of the Farmer's Wife cookie jar. Here are even more instructions for obtaining the perfect sugar cookie, as well as yet another variation of the recipe.*

# GRANDMOTHER'S COOKIE JAR

Mabel K. Ray, Foods Editor
*September 1931*

Can't you still see yourself standing on tip-toes in order to reach into grandmother's cookie jar on the first shelf in the pantry? And what surprises that jar held! Oatmeal, molasses, sugar, chocolate cookies, and lots of others found their way some time into it. No matter what kind they were, however, they were all *so* good.

I am going to give you recipes for a few of these old-fashioned cookies, starting off with soft sugar cookies which were special treasures in the old cookie jar. Their quality was partly a result of using an earthenware jar for storage, and of course, baking them to a delicate brown without drying them out helped also. Those were rolled on floured canvas, too. You ought to try that as the cookies don't stick to a floured cloth at all.

You say you have trouble with their browning only on the bottom? Well—possibly you have the ovens so full of pans that there is not much chance for the circulation of the heat up and around.

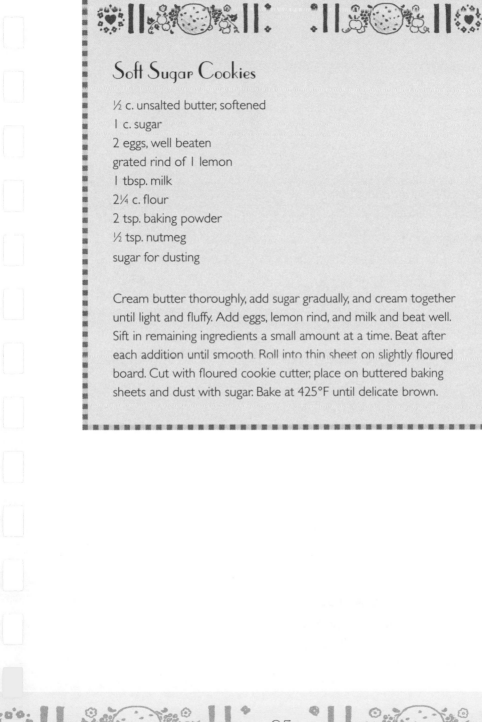

## Soft Sugar Cookies

½ c. unsalted butter, softened
1 c. sugar
2 eggs, well beaten
grated rind of 1 lemon
1 tbsp. milk
2¼ c. flour
2 tsp. baking powder
½ tsp. nutmeg
sugar for dusting

Cream butter thoroughly, add sugar gradually, and cream together until light and fluffy. Add eggs, lemon rind, and milk and beat well. Sift in remaining ingredients a small amount at a time. Beat after each addition until smooth. Roll into thin sheet on slightly floured board. Cut with floured cookie cutter, place on buttered baking sheets and dust with sugar. Bake at 425°F until delicate brown.

## ❦ Combination Cookies

(Light and Dark)

¾ c. unsalted butter, softened
1 c. sugar
2 eggs
4 c. flour
3 tsp. baking powder

¼ tsp. salt
¼ c. milk
2 oz. bittersweet chocolate,
  melted
1 tsp. vanilla

Cream the butter and add the sugar slowly. Add eggs and beat well. Sift flour, baking powder, and salt and add alternately with milk. Divide the dough into two parts. To the first part add half of vanilla, to the second add chocolate and remaining vanilla. Place the dark dough on top of the light dough and roll thin. Cut and bake on buttered baking sheets at 350°F for 8–10 minutes.

## ❦ Rolled Chocolate Cookies

W. S., Illinois

1 egg, beaten light
1 c. sugar
¼ c. unsalted butter, melted
1 c. sour cream
2½ c. flour

1 tsp. baking soda
½ tsp. salt
4 tbsp. unsweetened
  cocoa powder

Add beaten egg to sugar and butter. Sift together dry ingredients and add alternately with sour cream to first mixture. Mix, roll out, cut, and bake at 350°F on buttered baking sheets for 10–15 minutes.

# ❧ The Cookies That Went to Market

2 eggs, well beaten
2 c. white sugar, plus extra for sprinkling
1 c. lard (full)
1 c. sweet milk (scant)
⅓ tsp. nutmeg
1 tsp. vanilla
1 tsp. baking soda
1 tsp. baking powder
4 to 5 c. pastry flour
raisins for decorating

Mix first eight ingredients and let stand overnight if possible (*in the refrigerator!*), since they will not need as much flour if you do. Mix with flour—start with 1 c. and increase gradually as necessary to get a dough as soft as you can easily handle on the board. If too stiff, add cream. Roll out on a floured board and cut with cutters. Lay on buttered baking sheets with two raisins on top of each cookie and a sifting of white sugar. Bake at 400°F till done.

# ❧ Jumbles

*According to the* Penguin Companion to Food, *the original English jumbles of the seventeenth and eighteenth centuries were often tied in knots before baking. Here is a later interpretation of the biscuit, adapted from* The Pennsylvania Dutch Cook Book.

1 c. unsalted butter, softened
2 c. sugar
2 eggs
2 c. flour
Grated juice and rind of 1 lemon
1 c. grated unsweetened cocoanut

Cream butter and sugar; add eggs. Sift in flour, then add lemon juice, rind, and cocoanut. Roll thin on a board sprinkled with confectioner's sugar. Cut with cutters and place on buttered baking sheets. Bake at 350°F for 8–10 minutes.

## Apees

*A strangely controversial cookie. Dispute abounds over the origin of its name and the spelling (Apeas, Apise, A.P.s). Some claim the cookie should incorporate caraway seeds. Some list ingredients and instructions that match those for Sand Tarts (see Christmas Cookies, pg. 123). At any rate, a classic. Here is a "spiced" version of the sort that would have appealed to the farmer's wife.*

¾ lb. unsalted butter, softened
2¾ c. sugar
4 eggs
½ c. heavy cream
4 c. flour
2 tbsp. baking powder
2 tsp. cinnamon
⅛ tsp. each grated nutmeg and mace

Cream the butter and sugar; add the eggs and cream and stir well. Sift in the flour and baking powder, mix well, and add cinnamon, nutmeg, and mace. Roll out very thin on a floured board. Cut in shapes and place on unbuttered baking sheets. Bake at 350°F for 8–10 minutes.

# ❧ Corn-Sirup Buckwheat Cookies

*A wartime treat, making substitutes for scarce sugar and wheat flour.*

½ c. unsalted butter, softened
1 c. corn sirup
1 egg, well beaten
½ tsp. baking powder

1 tsp. cinnamon
1 tsp. ground cloves
¼ tsp. salt
2¾ c. buckwheat flour

Cream butter. Add the corn sirup and then the egg. Sift the remaining ingredients together and then add to the wet. Roll the dough thin, cut in shapes with a cutter, and bake on buttered baking sheets at 350°F, until done.

# ❧ Graham Cookies

2 c. honey
1 c. unsalted butter
1 c. sugar
2 eggs
1 c. buttermilk

1 tbsp. baking soda
1 tbsp. vanilla
4 c. graham flour
white flour as necessary
    to make a soft dough

Warm the honey and butter to the temperature of blood (*over a low heat till the butter is melted will do!*); then add sugar and eggs. Stir well, then dissolve soda in buttermilk. Add with vanilla and stir all well, then add graham flour and enough white flour to make a soft dough. Roll out on a floured board and cut. Bake at 350°F till done.

# ❦ Rolled Fruit Cookies

1 c. unsalted butter, softened

2 c. sugar

3 eggs, slightly beaten

1 tsp. cinnamon

1 tsp. ground cloves

⅓ tsp. baking soda

2 tsp. baking powder

3 tbsp. cold coffee or fruit juice

1 c. raisins, chopped and dredged in a little flour

up to 3 c. flour, to make a soft dough

Cream butter and sugar. Add eggs and beat until light. Sift in spices, baking soda, and baking powder with ½ c. flour and beat well. Add the coffee, then the raisins. Beat all together, then add remaining flour, ½ c. at a time, to make a soft dough. Roll out on a floured board and cut. Place on buttered baking sheets and bake at 350°F for 15–20 minutes.

# ❦ Raisin Cookies

1 c. sugar
½ c. unsalted butter, softened
2 eggs, beaten
1 c. raisins, chopped
½ c. buttermilk
3 c. flour
1 tsp. baking soda
1 tsp. cinnamon
½ tsp. ground cloves
¼ tsp. nutmeg

Cream sugar and butter and add eggs. Mix in raisins and buttermilk, then sift in flour with baking soda and spices. Add more flour if necessary to make a stiff dough. Roll out thin on a floured board and cut with cutters. Sprinkle with sugar and place on buttered baking sheets. Bake at 400°F for about 12 minutes.

**Raisin Cookies**

# ❦ Hermits

*Mrs. J. O. F., Utah*

*Try this recipe the* Farmer's Wife *way: Mix wet ingredients, then sift together dry (minus flour). Incorporate, then add only as much sifted flour as necessary to make a dough stiff enough to roll out.*

1 c. molasses, warmed
1 c. sugar, dissolved in molasses
1 c. unsalted butter, softened
1 c. buttermilk
1 c. raisins, chopped
1 egg
2 tsp. baking soda
pinch of salt
1 tsp. cinnamon
½ tsp. ground cloves
½ tsp. nutmeg
flour, sifted

Mix ingredients. Roll out to ½ inch thick on a floured board and cut with cutters. Place on buttered cookie sheets and bake at 350°F until lightly golden.

# ❦ Soft Molasses Cookies

1 c. unsalted butter

1 c. sugar

1 egg

2 tsp. baking soda dissolved in 1 c. buttermilk

2 c. molasses

8 c. flour, approximately—enough to make a soft dough
    that can be rolled out

1 tsp. salt

1 tbsp. ground ginger

1 tsp. cinnamon

Mix butter and sugar; add egg, then buttermilk mixture and molasses. Sift dry ingredients and add to mixture. Break dough in quarters to roll out, thick—⅜ of an inch—on a well-floured board, incorporating more flour as necessary in order to keep dough from sticking. Cut with round cutters and place on buttered baking sheets. Bake at 350°F for 6–10 minutes and remove to racks to cool. Do not let bottoms of cookies brown; these cookies will firm up as they cool, and they are meant to be *soft* cookies as opposed to something crisper, like molasses snaps.

*More scant (or nonexistent) instructions from the antique days of* The Farmer's Wife! *Dare you try your baking know-how with these?*

# Brown Cookies
*Rose Nisuander*

2 eggs
1 c. sugar
1 c. molasses
1 c. sour cream
⅔ c. unsalted butter
3 tsp. baking soda
1 tsp. each ground allspice, cloves, and cinnamon

# Good Ginger Cakes

1 pint molasses
1 c. white sugar
3 eggs
½ c. buttermilk
1 c. unsalted butter
2 tbsp. ground ginger
4 tsp. baking soda

Mix well and roll out on a floured board.

# ❦ Rolled Oats Cookies

1 c. unsalted butter, softened

2 c. sugar

1 tsp. baking soda

½ c. buttermilk

3 eggs, beaten

1 tsp. vanilla

½ c. light corn syrup

⅔ c. cooked rolled oats

6¼ c. flour, or enough for soft dough

2 tsp. baking powder

Cream butter and sugar. Put baking soda in buttermilk and add eggs. Combine with butter and sugar and beat well. Add vanilla, syrup, and cooked oats, then sift in flour and baking powder. Roll thin, since oats have a tendency to make cookies puff up thick. Place on buttered baking sheets, sprinkle with granulated sugar, and bake at 425°F until just done.

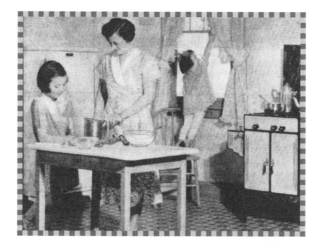

# ❦ Ginger Creams

2 c. molasses
1 c. unsalted butter
1 tbsp. ginger
1 tbsp. baking soda
4–6 c. flour

Mix ingredients well, being careful not to make dough too stiff. Roll out thick on a floured board and cut with a small cutter. Place on buttered baking sheets and bake at 325°F until just beginning to brown around edges (6–10 minutes)—take care not to scorch. Allow cookies to cool for a few minutes before removing to rack.

*Variations:*
1 tbsp. orange peel is a nice addition. Some add 1 tsp. black pepper.

Frost all with:
1 c. sugar
3 tbsp. hot water
2 egg whites, beaten

Cook first two ingredients on top of stove until they hair (230–234°F measured on a candy thermometer). When done, pour slowly into egg whites, beating all the while till cool. Spread on cookies.

## ❧ Nellie's Cookies

4 c. molasses
2 c. buttermilk
2 tbsp. baking soda
2 tbsp. ground ginger
5–8 c. flour
2 c. unsalted butter, softened

Bring molasses to a boil and add buttermilk, baking soda, and ginger. To this add all the flour necessary to make a stiff dough. Knead in butter. Roll out on a floured board and cut into desired shapes. Place on buttered baking sheets and bake at 350°F till done.

## ❧ Chocolate Krapfen

*Adapted from* Out of Vermont Kitchens

¾ c. sugar
¾ c. unsalted butter, softened
¾ c. hazelnut flour
¾ c. flour
2 squares bittersweet Baker's chocolate, grated
1 egg white

Cream sugar and butter. Mix in flours, then chocolate. Beat egg white stiff and fold into mixture. Roll out on lightly floured board to ¼ inch. Cut with small cutters and place on buttered baking sheets. Bake at 350°F till just done.

# ❦ Orange Butter Thins

*Adapted from* The Pennsylvania Dutch Cook Book

2 c. unsalted butter, softened
3½ c. confectioner's sugar
5 eggs
4 c. flour
1 tsp. baking soda dissolved in ½ c. sour cream
1 tsp. orange extract
¼ tsp. salt

Cream butter and sugar, then add eggs. Sift in the flour, then add baking soda in sour cream and extract. Roll out very thin on a floured board. Cut with cutters and place on buttered baking sheets. Bake at 350°F for about 10 minutes.

# ❧ Danish Brown Biscuits

*Another orange-flavored cookie, this one with almonds, adapted from the*
*Encyclopedia of European Cooking.*

½ c. molasses
¼ c. brown sugar
1 tbsp. unsalted butter
½ tsp. ground cloves
1 tsp. cinnamon
½ tsp. ground ginger
1½ tsp. grated orange rind
pinch baking soda
¾ c. flour
milk, for brushing
chopped blanched almonds
candied orange peel (see pg. 151), finely chopped

Heat molasses, sugar, butter, spices, and orange rind over low heat until
just warm. Add baking soda, then sift in flour. Mix well and roll out
very thin on a floured board. Cut into narrow rectangles and place on
buttered baking sheets. Brush with milk and decorate with almonds
and orange peel. Bake at 350°F for 8–10 minutes.

## ❦ Ginger Snaps

1 c. molasses, boiling hot
2 tbsp. vinegar
2 tsp. baking soda
2 tsp. ground ginger
1 egg, beaten
1 c. sugar
2½ c. bread flour

Add to molasses the vinegar, baking soda, ginger, and a little of the flour. Cool, then add remaining ingredients, sifting in dry ingredients. Chill in the refrigerator. Roll out very thin. Cut with cutters and place on buttered baking sheets. Bake at 425°F for about 6 minutes.

*Variations (and they are modest, not effecting any tremendous difference in flavor or texture):*

Dutch Molasses Snaps: Substitute ⅓ c. brown sugar for ¼ c. molasses.

Plain Molasses Snaps: Add ½ tbsp. softened unsalted butter and ½ tsp. cinnamon. Omit vinegar and 1 tsp. baking soda.

# ❦ Gingerbread of the French Fair

*Gingerbread of the French Fair—hard, spicy little cakes—may be baked in balls after the fashion of the old English goodies called gingernuts. Or the same dough may be rolled thin and cut for crisp, dark gingerbread men. It is a simple formula without eggs. The anise and coriander seed may be omitted, though they add much to the flavor of these peppery rounds.*
*—The Farmer's Wife Magazine*

½ c. unsalted butter
2 tbsp. ground ginger
2 tbsp. allspice
1 tbsp. mixed anise seed and ground coriander seed
grated rind of 1 lemon
1 c. molasses
3¼ c. pastry flour
2 tbsp. dried cherries, finely chopped
2 tbsp. citron, finely chopped
   (*Editorial note: better yet, candied orange and lemon peel, see pg. 151*)
2 tbsp. currants, finely chopped

Add butter, spices, and lemon rind to molasses and warm on stove until butter is melted, stirring constantly. Sift in flour, mix, and let stand off the heat for 20 minutes. Work in fruit and roll out on floured board to 1 inch. Cut with gingerbread men cutters and place on buttered baking sheets. Bake at 350°F for 20–25 minutes.

## ❧ Lemon Snaps

1 c. sugar
⅔ c. unsalted butter, softened
½ tsp. baking soda
2 tsp. hot water
flour, about 3 c.
lemon extract

Mix well, adding only enough sifted flour to make a dough stiff enough to roll. Roll thin on a floured board. Cut with cutters and bake at 325°F until golden.

---

## ❧ Oatmeal Snap Cakes

½ c. fine oatmeal
2 c. flour
pinch of salt
2 tbsp. sugar

2 tsp. baking powder
1 egg, beaten light
½ c. heavy cream
½ c. milk

Put oatmeal and flour in a bowl with the salt, sugar, and baking powder. Add cream and milk to the egg and stir together. Add to flour mixture. With a fork, make all into a light dough. Roll out on a floured board till thin and bake at 350°F till done. On account of the natural heaviness of the oatmeal, the baking powder is necessary.

# Gingersnaps

1½ c. unsalted butter, softened
1½ c. sugar
1 c. maple syrup
2 eggs
4½ c. flour
2½ tsp. baking soda
2 tsp. cinnamon
2 tsp. ground cloves
4 tsp. ground ginger
½ c. sugar mixed with 1 tbsp. cinnamon, for rolling

Cream butter with sugar, then add syrup and eggs. Sift in flour, baking soda, and spices. Cover bowl and refrigerate till stiff, then break off bits of dough and form into 1-inch balls. Roll in cinnamon and sugar and place on buttered baking sheets with plenty of room between. Bake at 350°F for 12–15 minutes.

# ❧ Hickory Nut Snaps

1½ c. molasses
1 tbsp. ground ginger
pinch salt
½ c. brown sugar
½ c. unsalted butter, softened
dash red pepper
1 c. hickory nuts, chopped
1 heaping tsp. baking soda dissolved in ½ c. hot water
3 to 4 c. flour
sugar for dusting

Mix first six ingredients in a deep saucepan and beat together smoothly; boil until quite thick. Remove from stove, and when just warm, add nuts, baking soda mixture, and enough flour to make a stiff dough, sifting in 1 c. at a time. Roll thin on a floured board and cut in fancy shapes. Place on buttered baking sheets and sprinkle with sugar. Bake at 425°F until done.

# ❦ Almond Snaps

*Adapted from* The Pennsylvania Dutch Cook Book

1 c. unsalted butter, softened
1 c. confectioner's sugar
4 egg yolks
3 tbsp. heavy cream
3 c. flour

Cream butter and sugar, then add eggs and cream. Sift in flour and mix. Roll very thin on a board dusted with confectioner's sugar. Cut with cutters and place on buttered baking sheets. Bake at 325°F till just golden. Then ice with:

2 egg yolks
2 tbsp. water
confectioner's sugar to thicken
2 c. blanched almonds, finely chopped.

Mix first three ingredients to a thick paste and brush onto cookies, then sprinkle with almonds. Return to oven briefly to help set icing.

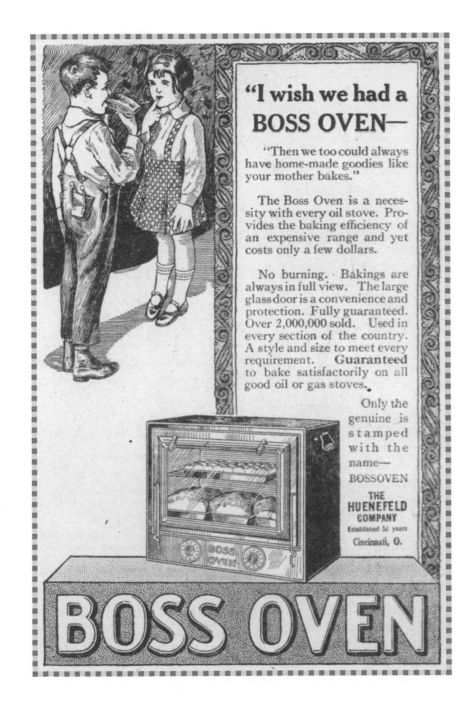

# BOUQUETS AND COOKIES
## May 1930

Five Minnesota women had just been publicly recognized as Master Farm Homemakers. In turn, each was expressing her appreciation of the honor and talking to the friends assembled.

Said Mrs. Charles E. Wirt of Lewiston: "I did not plan to be a farmer's wife. When we arrived at our new farm home we did not find the ordinary congratulations. It was all sympathy for my husband. My friends offered me the same sympathy. As we came to our front door, we found tied to the knob a Buckeye Cook Book and a year's subscription to *The Farmer's Wife*. In that *Farmer's Wife* I found a recipe for sour cream cookies which I tried. It was the only real success in baking that I had that year. I thought perhaps readers of *The Farmer's Wife* would like that recipe I tried 20 years ago."

"You'd better get that recipe." It was the banker on my left nudging my arm. "I'd like it myself," said the girl with the diamond at my right. And people across the way smiled their approval.

So we present the recipe. Here's luck to all of the 1930 farm brides, and may they find us as helpful a friend as did Mrs. Wirt years ago when the sour cream cookies made their debut!

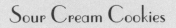

## Sour Cream Cookies

2 tbsp. shortening
2 c. white sugar
2 tbsp. butter
2 eggs
1 c. sour cream
flour
1 tsp. baking soda
1 tsp. baking powder

Cream shortening, add sugar and mix well with butter, add well beaten eggs, sour cream, and 2 c. of flour with baking soda sifted in. Add enough more flour to make a soft dough. Roll and cut and bake in a hot oven (400°F).

# ❦ Sour Cream Cocoa Cookies

1 egg, beaten light
1 c. sugar
¼ c. unsalted butter, melted
1 c. sour cream
2½ c. flour
1 tsp. baking soda
½ tsp. salt
¼ c. unsweetened cocoa powder

Add beaten egg to sugar and butter. Combine dry ingredients. Add dry ingredients and sour cream alternately to first mixture. Roll out, cut, and bake at 375°F till done.

## *Variation:*

Drop Cookies: Decrease the flour in the above recipe to 2 c. and drop dough by the teaspoonful on greased sheet. Ice with chocolate powdered icing sugar:

Combine 1 c. sifted confectioner's sugar with 2 tbsp. unsweetened cocoa powder, ¼ tsp. vanilla, and 1 tbsp. milk in a bowl. Stir in additional milk, 1 tsp. at a time, until icing is thin enough to drizzle.

# ❦ Sour Cream Molasses Cookies

| | |
|---|---|
| 1 c. unsalted butter | 2 tsp. baking soda |
| 1 c. brown sugar | 1½ tsp. salt |
| 1 c. molasses | 1½ tsp. ground ginger |
| 3 eggs, beaten | 3 tsp. cinnamon |
| 1 c. sour cream | up to 6 c. flour |

Cream butter with sugar, then add molasses, eggs, and sour cream. Sift baking soda together with salt, ginger, cinnamon, and 1 c. flour and mix into dough. Add more flour 1 c. at a time to make a soft batter. Chill dough several hours, then roll out on a floured board and cut with cutters. Place on buttered baking sheets and bake at 350°F for 12–15 minutes.

**To vary you may ice with:**
½ c. sugar
1½ tbsp. water
1 tbsp. unsalted butter
few drops vanilla

Boil together the first three ingredients to soft-ball stage (234–240°F registered on a candy thermometer). Whisk until cool and creamy, then add vanilla and spread on cookies.

For Sour Cream Molasses Bars: Spread the batter without chilling in a shallow buttered pan and bake at 350°F. While still warm, dust with powdered sugar. Cut in bars when ready to serve.

# Scotch "Dainties" and Shortbread

*Shortbread is a crumbly Scottish specialty that traditionally incorporates three ingredients: flour, sugar, and butter. Variations on this simple mixture range from lemon peel to spices to eggs.*

## Scotch Short Bread

3 c. flour
1 c. sugar
2 c. butter
1 oz. blanched almonds

Sift the flour twice and rub in the butter with the hands. Add the sugar and knead and mix either on a board or in a bowl until a dough is formed. Do not add either egg or milk, since the butter softens the mixing and will bind the ingredients together. Roll the dough rather thinly, cut into rounds or ovals, and press a few almonds onto each. Bake in a pie pan at 300°F until golden brown.

# ❦ Cinnamon Shortbread

*Adapted from* The Meetinghouse Cookbook

| | |
|---|---|
| 1 c. unsalted butter, softened | 3 egg yolks |
| ½ c. sugar | 1 egg white, lightly beaten |
| 3 c. flour | ½ c. sugar mixed with |
| ¼ tsp. nutmeg | 1 tbsp. cinnamon, for dusting |

Cream butter and sugar. Sift in flour and nutmeg and mix until smooth, then add egg yolks. Roll thin on a floured board and cut with cutters. Place on buttered baking sheets, brush with egg white, and sprinkle with cinnamon and sugar. Bake at 375°F for 12–15 minutes until lightly browned around edges.

# ❦ Dutch Shortbread

*Adapted from* The Pennsylvania Dutch Cook Book

| | |
|---|---|
| 1 c. unsalted butter, softened | 3 c. flour |
| ⅔ c. sugar mixed with grated | pinch salt |
|    rind of 1 lemon | 1 egg white, slightly beaten |
| 1 egg | ½ c. sugar mixed with 2 tbsp. |
| 6 hardboiled egg yolks, |    cinnamon, for dredging |
|    pressed through a sieve | |

Cream butter and add sugar mixture. Beat in whole egg, then add egg yolks. Sift in flour and salt and mix well. Roll dough into small balls and flatten. Dip in egg white and roll in cinnamon and sugar. Place on buttered baking sheets and bake at 325°F until golden.

## ❧ Shrewsbury Cakes

*A very old shortbread-type recipe from England rather than Scotland, in this adaptation from* The United States Regional Cook Book, *incorporating nutmeg; a little cinnamon may be added as well.*

½ c. unsalted butter, softened
½ c. sugar
1 egg
¼ tsp. nutmeg
¼ tsp. salt
2½ c. flour

Cream butter and sugar, then add egg, nutmeg, and salt. Sift in flour and mix well, then cover and refrigerate several hours. Roll out very thin and cut with cutters; place on buttered baking sheets. Bake at 350°F for 12–15 minutes.

## ❧ Scotch Dainties

*Mrs. Carl McAllster*

**To make Oatmeal Cookies:**

2 c. fine oatmeal
1 c. flour
1½ c. unsalted butter, slightly softened

½ tsp. baking soda dissolved in a little hot water
milk

Work first three ingredients until well mixed. Add baking soda and milk to make into a dough soft enough to roll out. These should be rolled thin on a floured surface and cut with a sharp knife or cooky cutter. Place on buttered baking sheets and bake at 350°F until lightly golden.

## To make Oatmeal Perkins:

| | |
|---|---|
| 1 c. brown sugar | 2 c. rolled oats |
| 1 c. unsalted butter, | 2 tsp. ground ginger |
|   softened | ½ tsp. ground cloves, |
| ¾ c. molasses |     cinnamon, or allspice |
| ½ c. water | ½ tsp. baking soda |
| 1½ c. flour | |

Make into cooky dough. Roll out thin and cut out in cooky fashion. Place on buttered baking sheets and bake at 350°F till done.

## To make Scotch Shortbread:

| | |
|---|---|
| 3 c. unsalted butter | 1 c. light brown sugar or powdered sugar |
| 4 c. flour | lemon peel, in small pieces |

Heat butter until soft but not melted. Add flour and sugar, knead about 30 minutes, then roll out on a floured board until dough is ½ inch thick. Cut in squares and place a piece of lemon peel on each square. Line cookie sheet with buttered wax or parchment paper and bake until done in a very slow oven—250–300°F. All Scotch folk love this, especially for a Christmas dainty. It is really a national confection.

## ❦ Filled Cookies

| | |
|---|---|
| 1 c. sour cream | ½ tsp. baking soda |
| 2 c. sugar | ¼ tsp. salt |
| 3 c. flour | 1 tsp. vanilla |

Blend the sour cream and sugar; sift in flour, baking soda, and salt, then add vanilla. Place a portion of the dough on a well-floured board and roll thin. Cut to desired size with a cutter that has been dipped in flour. Do not put the floured scraps together at the last. The flour that adheres to the scraps will make a stiffer dough and a less tender cooky.

A large variety of filled cookies may be made by using this recipe with different cooked fillings. After the cookies have been cut, put a small amount of cooked filling in the center of one cooky and place another cooky on top of it. Press the edges together and bake at 400°F till nicely golden.

**Raisin Filling:**

| | |
|---|---|
| 1 c. raisins, chopped | ½ c. water |
| ½ c. sugar | 1 tsp. flour |

Cook in a double boiler until thick. Cool before spreading on cooky.

### Fig Filling:

| | |
|---|---|
| 1½ c. dried figs, chopped | ½ c. water |
| | ⅓ c. sugar |

Mix in the order given and cook in a double boiler until thick. Cool before spreading.

### Date Filling:

| | |
|---|---|
| 1½ c. dates | ¼ c. water |
| ⅓ c. sugar | |

Wash dates and remove pits, if there are any. Add sugar and water and cook as above. Cool before spreading.

### Apricot Filling:

| | |
|---|---|
| 1 c. dried apricots, chopped | ¾ c. water |
| ¼ to ⅓ c. sugar, depending on how tart you like it | |

Place ingredients in saucepan and cook over low heat until thick and smooth, adding more water if necessary. Cool before spreading.

### Jam Filling:

Use spoonfuls of jam or preserves of your choosing.

### Apple Filling:

| | |
|---|---|
| 1 c. apple, chopped | ½ c. sugar |
| 1 tbsp. preserved ginger, chopped | juice and grated rind of 1 orange |
| | ½ c. nuts, chopped |

Mix and cook until thick and apples are clear. Roll out dough thin and cut half in rounds, half in 2½-inch squares. For the round cookies, put filling on half of the circles and top with the other half, crimping the edges with a fork. Of the squares, make filled crescents. Put a strip of the filling across one corner. Roll the dough over and over to make a filled roll. Shape as a crescent, with the filling showing at each end.

## ❦ Cream Cookies

*A sort of shortbread sandwich, adapted from* Favorite Recipes of the King's Daughters and Sons.

1 c. unsalted butter, softened
⅓ c. heavy cream
2 c. flour

Photo credit: Shutterstock

Mix ingredients and chill. Roll out as thinly as possible and cut in rounds. Sprinkle both sides with sugar, then place on buttered baking sheets and prick with a fork. Bake at 375°F for about 8 minutes, till lightly golden. Put together in pairs with:

¼ c. unsalted butter, softened
¾ c. confectioner's sugar
1 egg yolk
¼ tsp. vanilla

Blend together and spread on cookies.

# TABLE TALK
## Conducted by Mrs. Sarah A. Cooke
### *February 1913*

**Mrs. Woodrow Wilson's Old-Fashioned Cakes, Gingerbread and Cookies.** The charmingly domestic future mistress of the White House understands the art of cooking as well as she does the art of painting, the art of landscape gardening and the art of fine needlework, for which she is proficient in all these arts, which goes to prove that she is a marvelously well-rounded woman. Her domesticity is one of her chief charms, she is a homemaker in every sense of the word and a fine feminine figure, worthy to stand forth as an example to the women of the land.

She typifies to perfection the spirit of a great republic and is the ideal woman of democracy: many-sided, accomplished to a rare degree, gracious, warm-hearted and home-loving.

She is a southerner by birth, but has lived over half her life in the north. She, however, retains her native southern love of cooking, for in the South cooking is regarded as a fine art. She can make the most delicious things to eat and when she was first married she did her own cooking. Her cooks she trains herself, for her recipes are very fine and she knows exactly how they should be carried out.

Her cakes, cookies and gingerbread are delicious and here are the recipes.

## Old-Fashioned Cream Cookies

⅓ c. unsalted butter, softened
½ c. sugar
2 eggs
½ c. light cream

3–5 c. flour
2 tsp. baking powder
1 tsp. salt
2 tsp. ground ginger

Cream the butter, add the sugar, eggs, and cream. Into the mixture add 3 c. flour sifted together with the remaining ingredients, adding more if necessary to make a stiff dough; chill 20–30 minutes. Roll on a floured board as thin as possible, using a small part of the dough at a time. Cut into shapes and bake in a moderate oven (325–350°F) till done.

## Cinnamon Cookies

4 c. molasses
4 oz. unsalted butter
2 tbsp. cinnamon
2 c. buttermilk

1 tbsp. baking soda dissolved
   in ¼ c. cold water
8 c. flour

Put the molasses, butter, and cinnamon into a saucepan; heat gently, then add the buttermilk. Add baking soda. Remove from fire and when cool, add the flour. Roll out, using enough flour to prevent sticking. Cut into shapes, lay on buttered sheets, and bake till ready in a moderate oven (350°F).

## Maple Syrup Cookies

3 c. maple syrup
heaping cupful unsalted butter
4 eggs, separated

1 c. milk
2 tsp. baking powder
flour

Warm the maple syrup until it will melt the butter. Allow to cool, then add beaten egg yolks and milk. Finally, sift in baking powder with some flour, then fold in the egg whites beaten stiffly, then the remaining flour to make a stiff dough. Roll out, cut with cutters, lay on floured sheets, and bake in a moderate oven (350°F) till golden.

# Christmas Cookies

*The Farmer's Wife* and all her available relations were busy during the holiday season: mixing, rolling, cutting, dredging, frying, and decorating cookies of all varieties, to eat at home and to give as gifts. There were jobs for all, and cookie recipes certain to delight just about everyone.

# AT CHRISTMAS MAKE GOOD CHEER!
### Each and Every One May Lay a Fagot on the Yuletide Fire

*December 1916*

Dear Martha:

I have your letter asking me to do some Christmas shopping for you and I write to say that I decline your commission! You give me a list of friends and relatives here in town and the sums you can spend on each, and you breathe a sigh that the University for the children and the cost of the new silo have made the sum so small and then you ask me to get the best things I can find for the money. My gift, you are making.

My dear, you made my gift last summer, you and your intimate friend Nature, and I am returning your check, for you made most of these other gifts at the same time. . . . My dear, don't you see how you could so easily send yourself and your life and your own surroundings to each of us who are city-bound here? . . . It will cost you no more worry than a morning's selection and an afternoon's packing and no more money than parcel-post charges.

Alice has had a pretty hard time this year; that long illness has not left much surplus for Christmas dainties. So tuck a little butter or some eggs into a dressed fowl; or a wee young pig would not be a bit too much holiday jollity for her. Or, send doughnuts, filled cookies or ginger bread—you make them so well and they are so good. . . .

I've finished my lecture and I'm hoping that you will find it as palatable as I shall your goodies. I shall send you the most citified gift I can find because that is I and I am anticipating that mine from you will be redolent with the sunshine and pure air and peace that are *you!*

Your very best friend, —Mary

## Sand Tarts

*The classic Christmas cookie.*

| | |
|---|---|
| 1 c. unsalted butter, softened | 3½ c. flour |
| 1½ c. sugar | ½ tsp. cinnamon |
| 2 eggs | ¼ c. granulated sugar mixed with 1 tsp. cinnamon |

Cream butter and sugar, add the beaten eggs, and sift in dry ingredients. Roll very thin, brush with egg white, and sprinkle with cinnamon and sugar. Place on buttered baking sheets and bake quickly at 400°F. Citron, raisins, orange peel, blanched almond slivers, pecan halves, or maraschino cherries make good decorations for these if wished.

*Variation:* Substitute brown sugar for white and add ¼ tsp. salt.

# OLD COUNTRY CHRISTMAS CAKES

By Sarah Gibbs Campbell
*December 1928*

From a good many European countries come the recipes for these delightful Christmas cakes with their spicy, fruity flavors, which seem to get better the older they are. It was an old world custom for friends and neighbors to exchange Christmas cakes and many of their descendants in America still cling to this delightful custom and also hand down the original recipes from generation to generation.

These little cakes taste wonderfully good with either tea or coffee throughout the winter, but to be truly Christmas cakes, they must be cut in many shapes, some graceful and appropriate, others grotesque and quaint—moon and stars, horses, dogs, sheep, and quaint little figures of boys and girls. Some families have inherited these cutters and sometimes they are to be found in the stores of small towns which were founded by German, Polish or Bohemian settlers, or in the department stores of larger cities. Some good cooks are able to depend on a sharp knife and their own artistic ability to accomplish amazing results. But whether they are plain round cakes or decorated ones, it is a great comfort to feel that there is a goodly supply of them safely hidden in a tightly covered stone jar long before the last rush of Christmas cooking.

The recipes given will supply a delightful variety and if the quantities seem too large, it is quite easy to make only a half or quarter of the amount, but before doing this, remember how long they will keep and what charming last minute gifts or remembrances they will make.

## Honey Cakes

1 lb. sugar
1 lb. honey
1 tsp. baking soda dissolved in 2 tbsp. water
1 lb. flour
¼ tsp. cloves
1 tsp. cinnamon
ground cardamom seed from 3 pods
juice and grated rind of 1 lemon
4 c. pecan meats
¾ c. ground lemon peel

Put the sugar and honey in a saucepan; heat until the sugar is dissolved and the boiling point is reached. Remove from the fire and pour the mixture into a large bowl. Add the baking soda, dissolved in the water, immediately. Then stir in the flour and the spices that have been sifted together, and the lemon juice and rind. Add the nuts and citron (all chopped fine), mix well, roll very thin, and cut. If dough is allowed to cool before rolling, the process will be very difficult. Allow cakes to stand overnight before baking. Bake at 350°F for 20–30 minutes, until just done.

## ❧ Snickerdoodles

*Adapted from* Hot Recipes

*A nineteenth-century Pennsylvania Dutch specialty, with possibly ancient origins. Some versions resemble Jumbles, others, Sand Tarts. According to the Penguin Companion to Food by Alan Davidson, to be authentic they should contain nutmeg, nuts, and raisins.*

| | |
|---|---|
| 1 c. unsalted butter, softened | ½ tsp. salt |
| 1½ c. sugar | ¼ tsp. nutmeg |
| 2 eggs | 1 c. walnuts and raisins, chopped fine |
| 2¾ c. flour | ½ c. sugar mixed with 1 tbsp. cinnamon, for dusting |
| 1 tsp. baking soda | |
| 2 tsp. cream of tartar | |

Cream butter and sugar, then add eggs. Sift in dry ingredients, then mix in nuts and raisins. Form into small balls, place on buttered baking sheets, and flatten; dust with cinnamon and sugar. Bake at 400°F for 8–10 minutes.

CONTRIBUTED BY HARRIET COATES

## Dutch Christmas Cakes

1 c. unsalted butter, softened
1 c. sugar
1 tsp. grated orange rind
6 tbsp. orange juice
4 5 c. flour

2 tbsp. sugar sifted with
1 tsp. cinnamon,
for sprinkling
2 tbsp. sugar mixed with ½ tsp.
grated orange rind, for sprinkling

Cream the butter and sugar, stir in the orange rind and juice, then work in the flour. The dough should be very stiff, so it is necessary to work in the last flour with the fingers. Chill, then roll very thin, cut, and sprinkle each cookie with the cinnamon and sugar. Sprinkle the tops of other cookies with grated, dried orange rind and granulated sugar. Place on buttered baking sheets and bake at 350°F till done.

## Molasses Cookies

½ c. lard
2¾ c. sugar
1 c. molasses
4 eggs, slightly beaten
2½ to 5 c. flour
¾ of a whole nutmeg, grated

1 tsp. cinnamon
1 tsp. ground cloves
1 tsp. mace
1 tsp. baking powder
¼ tsp. baking soda
1 qt. pecan meats

Cream the lard and sugar, add molasses and eggs. Then sift in 2 c. of flour with the spices, baking powder, and soda. Stir in the chopped pecans and enough additional flour to roll easily. Cut, place on buttered baking sheets, and bake at 350°F till just gold around the edges, watching closely, for these cakes burn easily.

# ❦ Old English Gingernuts

½ c. unsalted butter,
   softened
2 c. sugar
2 eggs
4 c. flour
2 tsp. ground ginger

1 tsp. each of cinnamon
   and ground cloves
½ c. walnuts, chopped
sugar for rolling
citron pieces or walnut
   halves for garnish

Cream butter and sugar, beat in eggs, then add the flour sifted with the spices. The dough will seem quite stiff. Shape into little balls with the fingers, roll them in granulated sugar, and press a piece of citron or half an English walnut into each. Place on buttered baking sheets and bake at 350°F till golden.

---

# ❦ "Pfeffer-Nuesse"

*The German name for the wildly diverse and widely dispersed (throughout Europe, anyway) ginger biscuit.*

3¾ c. brown sugar
1 tbsp. ground cloves
1 tbsp. cinnamon
1 tbsp. ground ginger

4 eggs
about 4 c. flour
2 tsp. baking powder

Mix the sugar and the spices well. Beat in eggs, then add 2 c. flour sifted together with baking powder. Work in more flour to make a very stiff dough. Roll on a floured board to ½ inch and cut with a tiny round cutter. Bake at 350°F until done. These little cakes, having neither shortening nor milk, will keep indefinitely.

# ❦ Ginger Spice Cookies

¼ c. unsalted butter

½ c. molasses

½ c. milk

4 c. flour, sifted

½ tsp. salt

1 tsp. baking soda

1 tsp. baking power

1 tsp. mixed spice (see pg. 48)

1 tsp. ground ginger

1 egg

1 c. sugar

Heat butter and molasses in saucepan over low flame until butter is melted. Add milk, beat well, pour into mixing bowl, and set aside to cool. Sift flour, salt, baking soda, baking powder, and spices together. Beat egg; add sugar; add to molasses. Stir flour in gradually to form a smooth dough. Cover the dough and let ripen an hour. The dough is like putty—little flour is needed for rolling. Roll out to ⅓ inch. Cut in rounds, oblongs, or fancy shapes. Bake on slightly greased pans at 350°F until a light brown color.

# German Springerle

*Mrs. A. W., Illinois*

*Another lovely specialty of the Pennsylvania Dutch, brought over, according to food historian Alan Davidson, from the German province of Swabia. This recipe from a Farmer's Wife reader varies from tradition, which would have the cookies infused with anise and lemon rind.*

*Springerle molds, or boards, are squares or rectangles of wood grooved with various designs. Some have one large image (a flower, a bird), some four or six smaller images. There also exist twelve- and sixteen-image springerle rolling pins. Whichever you use, be sure to flour it before each pressing or rolling to prevent the dough from sticking.*

| | |
|---|---|
| 7 eggs, separated | I square bittersweet |
| 3 c. powdered sugar | Baker's chocolate, grated |
| I tsp. grated nutmeg | 2 tbsp. unsalted butter |
| I tsp. cinnamon | I tsp. baking powder |
| I tsp. vanilla | I c. flour |

Beat egg yolks and sugar, spices, vanilla, chocolate, and butter, which has been slightly softened to facilitate mixing. Fold in egg whites beaten. Mix baking powder with half the flour and stir or knead into mixture. Turn onto well-floured board and knead in as much flour as dough will hold. Roll very thin and mold over single springerle mold or mold of any kind. Press dough on mold to make design distinct. Cut cakes out and lay them on the table. Cover with clean cloth and let dry until morning. Place on buttered baking sheets and bake at 325°F for about 20 minutes.

# Norwegian Krum Kake

*Mrs. W. J., Minnesota*

*This recipe requires a krumkake iron, a contraption resembling a waffle iron that sits atop a stove burner and embosses a slight design on the cookie as it "bakes." The cookie is then rolled into a cone shape while warm. Not just for Christmas—but the holidays are a good excuse for the effort.*

| | | |
|---|---|---|
| 1 c. unsalted butter, melted | 2 c. flour | 1 tsp. vanilla |
| 1¾ c. sugar | 6 eggs | 1 c. cold water |

Mix ingredients to remove lumps and bake on krumkake iron until golden. Remove and roll out right away.

---

# St. Nicholas Cookies

*Adapted from* The United States Regional Cook Book

| | |
|---|---|
| 2 c. unsalted butter, softened | ½ tsp. each nutmeg and ground cloves |
| 2 c. sugar | ½ tsp. baking soda |
| 4 c. flour | ¼ tsp. salt |
| 4 tsp. cinnamon | ½ c. sour cream |

Cream butter and sugar, then sift in dry ingredients, adding alternately with sour cream. Mix well, shape into a log, wrap in wax paper, and refrigerate till stiff. Slice in ¼-inch rounds and place on buttered baking sheets. Bake at 400°F for 7–10 minutes, until nicely browned.

## ❦ Norwegian Kringler

*Adapted from* The United States Regional Cook Book

*The farmer's wife made kringler in 1928: braided, raised yeast cookies spiked with lemon rind and sprinkled with chopped blanched almonds. This yeast-less recipe for kringler is adapted from* The United States Regional Cook Book *and includes almond extract, raisins, and candied lemon peel, to approximate the recipe the farmer's wife would have baked some eighty years ago.*

| | |
|---|---|
| 1 c. sugar dissolved in 1 c. sour cream | ½ tsp. almond extract |
| 3 c. flour | 1 c. white raisins, slightly floured |
| 1 tsp. salt | strips of candied lemon peel |
| ¾ tsp. baking soda | to garnish (pg. 151) |

Sift dry ingredients into sour cream mixture. Stir in extract and raisins. Mix well and drop by teaspoonfuls onto buttered baking sheets. Bake at 350°F for 10–12 minutes, till lightly browned. While still warm, garnish with strips of candied lemon peel.

## ❦ Viennese Almond Cookies

| | |
|---|---|
| ½ c. unsalted butter, softened | ½ c. almond flour, plus more for rolling |
| 1¾ c. flour | 2 egg yolks |
| ½ c. sugar, plus more for rolling | 2 to 2½ tbsp. cream |

Work butter into flour until mealy (finer than for pie crust). Add sugar and almond flour and mix well. Add beaten yolks, then cream. Dough should be soft enough to handle without breaking. For "horseshoes," roll in long strips about the thickness of a pencil. Cut in 3-inch lengths and shape each piece as a crescent or horseshoe. Place on buttered baking sheet and bake at 400°F about 15 minutes. While warm, roll in a mixture of sugar and almond flour.

Cover ends with a thin chocolate icing made by melting 1 square bittersweet Baker's chocolate with 1 oz. unsalted butter, allowed to cool slightly before use.

*Variation:*
For jelly circles, roll dough quite thick, about ½ inch. Cut out very small rounds with a tiny cutter or wine glass. Make a dent in the center and put in a fleck of bright jelly. Sprinkle ground nuts and sugar around edge. Bake at 400°F for 10 to 15 minutes.

## ❦ Almond Pretzels

*Adapted from* The United States Regional Cook Book

| | |
|---|---|
| 1 c. unsalted butter, softened | 1 c. sugar |
| 2½ c. flour | ½ tsp. salt |
| 6 eggs | 1 tbsp. milk mixed with 1 egg white |
| ¼ c. heavy cream | ½ c. blanched slivered almonds |
| 1 tsp. almond extract | |

Cut butter into flour until mixture resembles coarse meal. Mix in eggs, cream, extract, sugar, and salt. Refrigerate till firm, then form into 8-inch "pencils;" twist into pretzel shapes. Place on buttered baking sheets, brush with milk mixture, and sprinkle with almonds. Bake at 350°F for 12–15 minutes.

# THE CHRISTMAS SWEET TOOTH

By Helena Korte
*December 1924*

Our preparations for Christmas have never seemed complete without "all kinds" of cookies for the children. The prime favorites are a rather rich confection, slightly troublesome to make; but they are worth all the painstaking a perfect result demands. Grown people, as well as children, approve of them. The mixture calls for:

2 c. white sugar
1 c. unsalted butter
2 whole eggs
4 egg yolks
1 tsp. vanilla or other flavoring
1 large tbsp. vinegar
1 level tsp. baking soda
4–6 c. flour
powdered sugar, for dusting

No liquid is used except the vinegar. If milk or water is added, the dough will be easier to work, but the cookies will lose their characteristic quality and become ordinary. If the vinegar is extremely sour, it may be weakened slightly with water.

Cream the sugar and butter. Add the eggs well beaten and the flavoring. Put the vinegar into a cup; stir in the soda and, as it foams, add it quickly to the mixture and beat all together thoroughly. Work in sifted flour little by little to make a soft, smooth dough, as the dough is very sticky and crumbly, it can be more easily managed if only a part of it is rolled out at one time. Fill one set of baking pans, then take a fresh piece of dough and roll again, always keeping the board well floured. Cut out and place the rounds in pans so the edges do not touch. They should be about one-half inch apart to allow for rising and spreading. Sift a little powdered sugar over the cookies and bake them quickly in a rather hot oven, with care to prevent scorching. The work is easier if two can attend to it, one to roll and cut out the cookies, the other to watch the baking. When taken from the oven, they should be spread on a table covered with a clean, dry cloth and left until they are cool and crisp. Then they may be packed away until needed.

These cookies may be cut into any fanciful design as they are not crumbly after baking and will hold their shape well. For a special children's party this might be desirable. The plain rounds taste just as well, however, and if they are topped with stiff jelly or thick jam, just before serving, they appear sufficiently festive for any occasion.

If stored in a cool, dry place, the cookies will keep almost indefinitely—if allowed to. As time passes, they may seem to become very dry, but they soften at once in the mouth. Their greatest enemy is moisture.

## ❦ Almond Rings

*A spiced macaroon dressed up for the holidays, adapted from* The Pennsylvania Dutch Cook Book.

| | |
|---|---|
| 6 egg whites | 1 c. almond flour |
| pinch salt | 1 tsp. vanilla |
| 2 c. powdered sugar | granulated sugar, for sprinkling |
| ¼ tsp. nutmeg | |

Beat the egg whites with the salt until stiff. Gradually whip in the sugar, beating till thick and gluey. Fold in nutmeg, almond flour, and vanilla, then spoon batter onto buttered cookie sheets in ring shapes. Bake at 325°F until nicely golden. Sprinkle with sugar.

## ❦ Swedish Spritz Cookies I

*Mrs. A. J., Iowa*

1 c. unsalted butter, softened
1 c. sugar
1 egg
2 tsp. almond extract
2½ to 3 c. flour to make a stiff dough

Cream butter and sugar; add egg, extract, and flour. Force through a cookie press to form into rings or fancy shapes. Place on unbuttered baking sheets. Bake in a hot oven (400°F), taking care not to burn.

# Swedish Spritz Cookies II

2 sticks unsalted butter,
softened
⅓ c. sugar

3 egg yolks
1 tbsp. almond flour
2½ c. flour

Cream butter and sugar, add egg yolks, then almond flour and flour. Mix well. Force through cookie press into desired shapes and place on unbuttered baking sheets. Bake at 400°F for 6–10 minutes.

# Sandbakels

1 lb. unsalted butter, softened
1⅛ c. sugar

1 egg
4 c. flour

½ tsp. salt
1 c. almond flour

Cream butter and sugar, then add egg. Add remaining ingredients. Press small bits into cookie forms [traditionally, small fluted tart-like tins] and place on baking sheets. Bake at 350°F until delicately browned.

# Swedish Spritsbakelser

1 c. unsalted butter
1 c. sugar

1 egg
1 tsp. almond extract

2½ to 3 c. flour

Cream butter and sugar; add egg, extract, and flour. Dough must be forced through the cookie press and formed in rings or fancy shapes. Place on buttered baking sheets and bake at 400°F, taking care not to burn.

# ❦ Swedish Allspice Cookies

*This recipe makes a lot of cookies!*

¾ lb. unsalted butter, softened
2½ c. sugar
1 c. dark corn syrup
1 c. heavy cream
1 tbsp. cinnamon

1 tbsp. ground cloves
2 tsp. allspice
1 tbsp. baking soda
12 c. flour, approximately

Cream butter and sugar. Add corn syrup and mix in cream alternately with dry ingredients sifted together. Chill in refrigerator, then roll out very thin. Cut in Christmas trees, diamonds, or rounds, and place on buttered baking sheets. Bake at 375°F for about 10 minutes.

# ❦ Love Krandse

*Miss S. R., Nebraska*

1 c. unsalted butter, softened
½ c. sugar, plus extra for dipping
3 c. flour
4 egg yolks, hard-cooked and pressed through a sieve
1 tsp. vanilla
1 egg, lightly beaten

Cream butter and sugar and mix with flour. Add the egg yolks and vanilla. Roll the dough thin and form in small wreaths. Dip in beaten egg and sugar. Place on buttered cookie sheets and bake at 350°F till just done.

## ❦ Vanillekipferl (Vanilla Crescents)

*Adapted from* Out of Vermont Kitchens

½ c. unsalted butter, softened
¼ c. sugar
½ c. almond flour
3 c. flour
1 tsp. vanilla

Cream butter and sugar and add remaining ingredients. Roll out on lightly floured board to ¼ inch. Cut into crescent shapes and place on buttered baking sheets. Bake at 350°F until lightly golden.

- - - - - - - - - - - - - - - - - - - - - - - - - - - - - - - - - - - - - - -

## ❦ Kringla

| | |
|---|---|
| 1 stick unsalted butter, softened | 1 c. almond flour |
| ½ c. sugar | 3 c. flour |
| ½ c. brown sugar, packed | 1 tsp. baking soda |
| 2 tsp. vanilla | 2 tsp. baking powder |
| 1½ tsp. lemon peel, grated | 2 tsp. nutmeg |
| 1 egg | 1 c. sour cream |

Cream butter and sugars till light and fluffy, then add vanilla, lemon peel, and egg. Stir in almond flour, then sift in remaining dry ingredients, adding alternately with sour cream. Cover and refrigerate overnight. Roll out thinly in small amounts on a lightly floured board. Cut into strips 3½ inches long, roll into "pencils," then twist into figure eights. Place on buttered baking sheets and bake at 350°F for about 8 minutes, till lightly browned.

## ❦ Kovlouria

*Adapted from* Cohasset Entertains

3 sticks unsalted butter, softened
¾ c. sugar
3 eggs, plus 1 for brushing
1½ tsp. vanilla
½ c. heavy cream
3 c. flour
½ tsp. cinnamon
2½ tsp. baking powder
sesame seeds for sprinkling

Cream together butter and sugar, add eggs one at a time, then add vanilla and cream. Sift in dry ingredients and mix well. Form into small doughnut shapes and place on buttered baking sheets. Brush with beaten egg and sprinkle with sesame seeds. Bake at 350°F for 25–30 minutes, until lightly golden.

# Apricot Buttons

*Adapted from* The Meetinghouse Cookbook

½ c. dried apricots
⅔ c. sugar
½ c. unsalted butter, softened
1 egg, separated
½ tsp. vanilla
1 c. flour
½ tsp. salt
½ c. blanched almonds, chopped

Cover apricots with water and cook over medium-low heat until tender. Puree in blender with some apricot cooking liquid and ⅓ c. sugar. Return mixture to stove and cook slowly, stirring constantly, until thick. Cream butter with remaining sugar and add egg yolk and vanilla. Sift in flour and salt and shape dough into small balls. Dip in unbeaten egg white and roll in almonds. Place on buttered baking sheets with plenty of room between and imprint with thumbprints. Bake at 300°F for 30 minutes. Remove to cooling racks and fill centers with apricot mixture.

# CHRISTMAS CAKES AND CANDIES

By Mabel K. Ray
*December 1930*

What can I give Cousin Laura for Christmas? For the woman who makes lovely cakes and candies the question is easily answered, as no more acceptable gifts could be given to friends or relatives. In fact such gifts are especially suitable since they carry with them truly individual thoughts from the giver.

Interesting boxes for packaging Christmas gifts . . . can be made by selecting tin coffee cans about 5 inches high and 6 inches in diameter, boiling off the paint that is on them and then painting the outside some attractive color. You may also put on a neat design. Instead of painting, colored paper, such as envelope lining, might be pasted on the outside of the box, then shellacked. Oilcloth may be used instead of paper.

Pasteboard boxes of the correct size and style may also be bought inexpensively. If something a little grander is wished, small reed baskets filled with assorted cookies are attractive, and the basket will be just the thing to act as a sewing fitall.

Wax paper is needed to line the boxes and in some cases to wrap individual pieces. If more than one layer of . . . cookies is packed a thin piece of white cardboard, such as used for posters, or a heavy piece of white stationery, is good to separate the layers.

Packing the . . . cookies . . . in the box in a pleasing arrangement may seem very difficult at first. However, with a little practice and forethought as to color variations and shapes, the trick will soon be learned. No matter how one packs the

gift box or with what, a good rule to remember is to pack it so that the articles hold their positions and are not jumbled together upon arrival at their destination. What could be more disappointing than to have one's interest aroused by the outside of the package then inside find—just hash. After all that work and a good product to begin with, too!

After packing the container, wrap with Christmas tissue, and tie with cord or ribbon in harmony as to color with the gift box. If the box is to be given to a friend present in the home at Christmas or nearby a sprig of holly, mistletoe, evergreen or bittersweet may be tucked on top where the package is tied and lend much cheer.

## Christmas "Brownies"

| | |
|---|---|
| ½ c. unsalted butter, softened | 1 tsp. salt |
| 1 c. brown sugar | 2 tsp. baking powder |
| 1 c. dates or nuts, chopped | 1 tsp. cinnamon |
| ¼ c. rolled oats | ½ tsp. nutmeg |
| ½ c. milk | 2 c. flour |

Cream butter and sugar, then add nuts or dates and oats. Sift dry ingredients together and add to butter mixture alternately with milk. Drop by spoonfuls on buttered baking sheets and bake at 350°F till done.

## ❧ Caraway Cakes

1 c. light brown sugar

¼ c. unsalted butter, melted

1 egg

½ c. water

2 tbsp. caraway seeds soaked 10 minutes in water to cover,
   then drained

pinch salt

2 tsp. baking powder sifted together with 2 c. flour

Mix ingredients together, adding more flour if necessary to make a dough that may be rolled in the hand without sticking. Flour the hands and form into balls the size of walnuts, flatten, place on greased cookie sheets, and dust with granulated sugar. Bake at 350°F till golden.

## ❧ Moravian Brown Christmas Cookies

*Adapted from* The Pennsylvania Dutch Cook Book

| | |
|---|---|
| 1 c. brown sugar | 1 tsp. ground ginger |
| 1 c. unsalted butter | 5 c. flour |
| 1 tsp salt | 1 egg |
| 1 tbsp. cinnamon | 1 c. molasses, slightly warmed |
| ½ tsp. ground cloves | 1 tsp. baking soda dissolved in ¼ c. hot water |

Cream sugar and butter; sift in salt, spices, and 1 c. flour. Add egg and molasses, then stir in baking soda. Sift in remaining flour a little at a time to make a stiff dough. Mix well, cover, and refrigerate overnight.

Roll out very thin on a floured board and cut in Christmas shapes. Place on buttered baking sheets and bake at 325°F for 12–15 minutes.

■ ■ ■ ■ ■ ■ ■ ■ ■ ■ ■ ■ ■ ■ ■ ■ ■ ■ ■ ■ ■ ■ ■ ■ ■ ■ ■ ■ ■ ■ ■ ■ ■ ■ ■ ■

# ❦ Moravian Scotch Cookies

*Adapted from* The Pennsylvania Dutch Cook Book

| | |
|---|---|
| ½ c. unsalted butter, softened | 3 c. flour |
| ½ c. sugar | pinch salt |
| 1 egg | 1 tsp. caraway seeds |

Cream butter and sugar, add egg, then sift in flour and salt. Add caraway seeds and mix. Roll out very thin on a floured board and cut with cutters. Place to bake on buttered baking sheets and bake at 325°F for 12–15 minutes. Cool and frost with:

| | |
|---|---|
| 4 tbsp. water | 1 egg white |
| 1 c. sugar | colored sugar |

Boil the water and sugar until the syrup threads (230–234°F measured on a candy thermometer). Beat egg white till stiff, then beat in syrup. When thick and smooth, spread on cookies and sprinkle with colored sugar.

# GIFTS FROM YOUR COOK STOVE
## Better than Trinkets Bought in the Shops

By Annette C. Dimock
*December 1923*

The older I get the surer I am that people have a hankering for home-cooked Christmas gifts. This rule for ginger snaps makes half a bushel! So we call them:

## Half Bushel Snaps

5 c. molasses
1 c. boiling water
4 c. sugar
1 lb. butter
2 tbsp. cinnamon
2 tbsp. ground ginger

Put all ingredients into a saucepan and heat until the butter melts. Remove from fire and add 2 tbsp. soda. Cool. Add flour to make a dough which can be rolled very thin and finish like any cookies.

It matters less what we give as a Christmas greeting than the spirit in which we make our gifts. I once buried a hatchet by sending a birthday cake to a mere acquaintance who "had a mad" on. And we are now as good friends as at first. Let's scrap our hatchets and bake them into good things for our friends.

# Drop Cakes for Holiday Baskets

1 c. sugar (brown or white)
½ c. unsalted butter, softened
2 eggs
½ c. light sour cream
½ c. corn syrup
1 tsp. each cinnamon and
   ground cloves

1 tsp. baking soda (dissolved
   in 2 tbsp. hot water)
1 c. each raisins and figs
   or dates, chopped
2½ c. flour
½ tsp. baking powder
½ c. black walnuts

Cream the sugar and butter; add eggs, then sour cream and syrup. Next add the spices and soda dissolved in 2 tbsp. hot water. Mix fruit with ¼ c. flour to keep from settling. Add remaining flour and baking powder to the batter until stiff enough to drop, then stir in fruit and nuts and drop on buttered baking sheets. Bake at 350°F until golden brown.

# GOODIES FROM THE FARM
## Christmas Sweets in Dainty Packages

By Anna Coyle
*December 1922*

Christmas thoughts for the town friend take expression in numerous tempting morsels from the farm in gala holiday wrappings. There is a charming personality about these gifts.

Boxes or baskets of fancy cookies, a basket of candy, home-made grape juice, a jar of pickles or candied fruits with the jar top enameled and decorated: all these will find a warm welcome at the hearth of the city dweller who might otherwise not have the abundance of good things that link the present with memories of old time Christmases.

## Fancy Holiday Cookies

Stir up a batch of cookies according to a favorite recipe and proceed to stir up and roll out in the usual way. The cutting and decorating gives the suggestion of Christmas. Cut in the form of bells, sleighs, and Christmas trees. Decorate some with raisins, others with candied cherries cut in strips, nuts, or strips of candied orange peel. Bake to a golden brown and pack in boxes.

These in a box will be highly appreciated by the stay-at-home lady who delights in serving a cup of tea and dainty bite to her holiday callers.

## Chocolate Honey Rounds

½ c. unsalted butter, softened
⅓ c. sugar
⅔ c. honey
2 eggs
2 squares bittersweet Baker's chocolate,
    melted and left to cool slightly

3 c. flour
½ to 1 tsp. ground anise
½ tsp. baking soda
1½ tsp. baking powder
½ tsp. salt
2 or 3 tbsp. cream

Cream butter, add sugar and honey, then add eggs and cooled melted chocolate. Mix until very creamy. Sift in dry ingredients and add a little cream to blend. Shape into balls, place on buttered baking sheets, and stamp into rounds by flattening with a glass covered with a damp cloth. Bake at 350°F for about 10 minutes. These are better after storing a few days in a covered tin.

## Candied Orange and Lemon Peels

Candied orange and lemon peels make delicious garnishes for cookies. Remove the peel from twelve lemons or eight oranges and cut the peel in ¼-inch strips. Place in a saucepan and cover with cold water. Bring to a boil and boil 20 minutes. Drain and set aside. Make a syrup by combining 2 c. sugar with 1 c. water. Boil in a saucepan over high heat until syrup reaches thread stage (230°F on a candy thermometer), add the peel, simmer for 5 minutes, remove with a fork, and roll lightly in granulated sugar. Candied peel also adds variety to the holiday candy boxes.

Photo credit: Marcie Fowler/Shutterstock

# Bars and Squares

Part cake, part cookie, enjoyed by all, especially when they are gobbled still-warm out of the oven.

# BAKING INSURANCE

By Miriam J. Williams

*June 1936*

What happens when the oven isn't right? If it is quite a bit off toward the too-hot or too-cool side, the result is . . . heavy [cookies]. How to avoid failures and disappointments in baking is every homemaker's wish.

There is always the crusader for *the* one right way, no other method is right. There is not necessarily one right way of baking a certain product, for experiments may show that several methods are reasonably successful. The vote of the majority, however, will be for one, or perhaps two, methods which are the most satisfactory with average conditions.

Personal opinion will always enter in, of course, as to which [cookie] is the most satisfactorily baked. As for appearance, most judges vote for a fairly well-browned product. . . . Correct baking is important for good texture and flavor, too, and in the eyes of the judge, these are more important than appearance. Usually the three go hand-in-hand, that which looks really good . . . is equally pleasing in texture and taste.

In the May issue of *The Farmer's Wife Magazine* was an article on the importance of home baking in the farm woman's routine. Studies show that the average one is poorly equipped with baking guides, nor is she particularly time and temperature conscious. Suggestions were given as to the selection of baking pans, their placement in the oven and other important factors in baking. A reliable portable thermometer, preferably of the mercury type, was recommended as a wise investment for the woman who does not have a regulated oven.

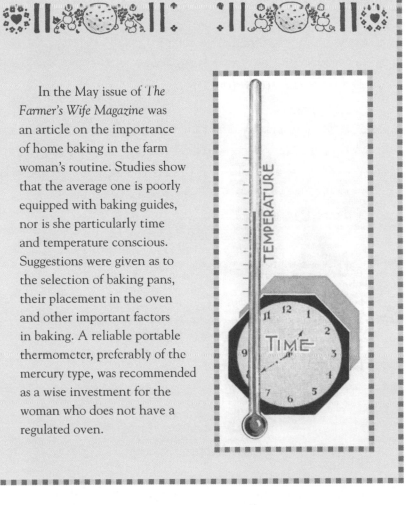

# ❦ Rolled Wafers

¼ c. unsalted butter, softened
½ c. confectioner's sugar
¼ c. milk

⅞ c. flour
½ tsp. vanilla

Cream butter; add sugar gradually and milk drop by drop. Add flour and vanilla. Spread very thinly with a broad, long-bladed knife or spatula on a buttered, inverted pan. Crease in 3-inch squares and bake at 300°F until delicately browned. Keep warm while squares are cut apart and quickly rolled up, jelly-roll style.

# ❦ Butter Bars

1 c. unsalted butter, softened
1 c. sugar, plus ¼ c. for sprinkling
1 egg, separated
2 c. flour
½ c. blanched almonds, finely chopped

Cream butter and 1 c. sugar, then add egg yolk. Sift in flour and mix well. Roll out to ¼ inch and lay out on unbuttered baking sheets. Brush with egg white and sprinkle with nuts and remaining sugar. Spread in buttered 8-inch-square baking pan. Bake at 300°F for 25–30 minutes. Cut in bars to serve.

For Cinnamon Butter Bars: To above recipe, add 2 tsp. cinnamon along with flour.

# ❦ Cocoanut Tea Cakes

1½ c. unsweetened shredded cocoanut
3½ c. flour
½ lb. unsalted butter, softened
2 eggs
¾ c. sugar

Mix all together and spread very thin in a buttered 8-inch-square baking pan. Bake at 300°F for about 10 minutes, till done. Cut in squares to serve.

# ❦ Graham Cracker Squares

*Adapted from* Recipes Tried and True by Cooks

½ c. unsalted butter, softened
¾ c. brown sugar
2 eggs
1 tsp. vanilla
1 c. flour
1 tsp. baking powder
½ tsp. salt
1 c. graham cracker crumbs
½ c. walnuts, chopped
½ c. unsweetened shredded cocoanut

Cream butter and sugar, then beat in eggs and vanilla. Sift in flour, baking powder, and salt, then mix in cracker crumbs, nuts, and cocoanut. Spread in buttered 8-inch-square baking pan and bake at 350°F for 25–30 minutes, till done. Cut in squares to serve.

## ❦ Walnut Squares

*Adapted from* Our Favorite Recipes

| | |
|---|---|
| 1 c. flour | 2 c. walnuts, chopped |
| pinch salt | 2 eggs |
| 2 c. brown sugar | 1 tsp. vanilla |

Mix all together and spread in a buttered 8-inch baking pan. Bake at 325°F till done. Cut in squares to serve.

---

## ❦ Pecan Bars

*Adapted from* Favorite Recipes of the King's Daughters and Sons

1 c. unsalted butter, softened
¾ c. sugar
1 egg
1 tsp. almond extract
2¼ c. flour
½ tsp. baking powder
pinch salt
1½ c. pecans, chopped
1 egg white

Cream butter and sugar, then add egg and almond extract. Sift in dry ingredients then mix in pecans. Spread in buttered 9x12-inch baking pan. Bake at 400°F for about 25 minutes, until done. Cool and cut in "fingers" to serve.

## ❧ Walnut Squares

*Adapted from* The Meetinghouse Cookbook

| | |
|---|---|
| 2 tbsp. unsalted butter | 1 c. brown sugar |
| ⅓ c. flour | 1 c. walnuts, chopped |
| ⅛ tsp. baking soda | 2 eggs |
| ⅛ tsp. salt | 1 tsp. vanilla |

Melt butter in a 9x12-inch baking pan. Sift together flour, baking soda, and salt, then mix in remaining ingredients. Pour over butter in pan and tap on countertop to settle. Cook at 350°F for 20–25 minutes, till done. Cool and cut in squares to serve.

## ❧ Almond Squares

*Adapted from* Cohasset Entertains

2 eggs, well beaten
1 c. sugar
1 c. flour
½ c. unsalted butter, melted
pinch salt
1 tsp. almond extract
½ c. blanched almonds, chopped

Add sugar to eggs and beat well. Add remaining ingredients, mix well, and spread in an 8-inch-square buttered baking pan. Bake at 350°F for 20–25 minutes. Cool and cut in squares to serve.

# ❧ Date Squares

1 c. unsalted butter, softened
2 c. brown sugar
2 eggs
2 c. dates, chopped
4 c. flour
½ tsp. salt
2 tsp. cinnamon
3 tsp. baking powder
1 tsp. nutmeg
⅔ c. milk
1 c. pecans, chopped
confectioner's sugar, for rolling

Cream butter and sugar, then beat in the eggs one at a time. Roll the dates in a little flour and sift all the dry ingredients together. Add the milk and flour alternately to the creamed mixture, then stir in the dates and pecans. Spread in a buttered 9x12-inch baking pan and bake at 325°F till firm. Cut in small squares while still hot and roll in confectioner's sugar. This recipe is perhaps a modern version of the old-fashioned date loaf.

# ❦ Date Bars

*A slight variation on the preceding recipe.*

| | |
|---|---|
| 1 c. sugar | ⅛ tsp. salt |
| 3 eggs | 40 dates, chopped |
| 3 tbsp. water | 1 c. walnuts, chopped |
| 1 c. flour | ½ c. confectioner's sugar, for rolling |
| 1 tsp. baking powder | |

Cream the sugar well with the eggs and mix with the water. Sift together the flour, baking powder, and salt and mix with dates and nuts. Combine with egg mixture. Spread in ½-inch-thick layer on buttered baking sheet. Bake at 350°F for 15–20 minutes, until firm to the touch. When cool, remove side crusts and cut in bars. Roll in confectioner's sugar just before serving.

# ❦ Raisin-and-Date Bars

| | |
|---|---|
| 1 c. sugar | 1 c. flour |
| 1 egg | 2 tsp. baking powder |
| 1 tsp. vanilla | ¼ tsp. salt |
| ¾ c. each raisins and dates, chopped | confectioner's sugar, for rolling |

Mix the sugar, egg, and vanilla. Mix the fruit and sifted dry ingredients and add to the first mixture. Turn into a buttered 8-inch-square baking pan and bake at 350°F for 30 minutes. Remove from the pan and when cool, cut into narrow strips about 1 inch wide and 4 inches long. Roll each strip in confectioner's sugar.

## ❧ Hermits

*Adapted from* American Cooking: New England

½ c. unsalted butter, softened
½ c. sugar
2 eggs
½ c. molasses
2 c. flour
1½ tsp. baking powder
1 tsp. cinnamon
½ tsp. ground cloves
¼ tsp. nutmeg
¼ tsp. salt
1 c. raisins, chopped
½ c. walnuts, chopped

Cream butter and sugar; mix in eggs, then molasses. Gradually sift in flour, baking powder, spices, and salt and mix well.

Dredge raisins and walnuts in a little flour and add. Spread mixture in a buttered, floured 9x12-inch baking pan and bake at 350°F for 12–18 minutes, till done. Cool and cut in squares to serve.

# ❦ Chocolatey Fruit & Nut Squares

| | |
|---|---|
| 1 c. dates, chopped fine | 1 c. sugar |
| 1 c. boiling water | 2 eggs |
| 1 tsp. baking soda | 1⅓ c. flour |
| 1 tsp. salt | 12 oz. semi-sweet chocolate chips |
| 1 tsp. vanilla | ¼ c. walnuts, chopped |
| 1 c. unsalted butter, melted | |

Mix all ingredients but chocolate and nuts and spread in buttered 8x10-inch baking pan. Cover with chocolate and nuts and bake at 350°F for 40 minutes. Cool and cut in bars to serve.

---

# ❦ Brownies

*Chocolate-free brownies! Today we'd call these blondies.*

⅔ c. brown sugar
⅔ c. unsalted butter, softened
4 eggs
⅔ c. molasses
2 c. flour
2 c. walnuts, chopped fine

Cream the sugar and butter, add the eggs and molasses, then the flour and nuts. Bake in a buttered square or small oblong pan at 350°F for 15–20 minutes. Cut in squares to serve.

# ❧ Apple Blondies

*Adapted from* Favorite Recipes of the King's Daughters and Sons

½ c. unsalted butter, softened
¾ c. sugar
1 egg
1 c. flour
½ tsp. baking powder
½ tsp. baking soda
1 tsp. cinnamon
⅛ tsp. nutmeg
1 c. apples, cored, peeled, and finely chopped
1 c. walnuts, finely chopped

Cream butter and sugar, add egg, then sift in flour, baking powder and soda, and spices. Mix in apples and walnuts and pour into buttered 8-inch-square baking pan. Bake at 350°F for 30–35 minutes. Cool and cut in squares to serve.

## ❦ Date Bars

*Adapted from* Favorite Recipes of the King's Daughters and Sons

¾ c. flour
¾ tsp. baking powder
pinch salt
1 c. dates, chopped
½ c. walnuts, chopped
2 eggs, well beaten
3 tbsp. unsalted butter, melted
¾ c. honey

Sift together first three ingredients and mix with dates and nuts. Mix eggs, butter, and honey and add to flour mixture. Mix well. Pour into buttered 8-inch-square baking pan and bake at 350°F for about 25 minutes, till done. Cut in bars to serve.

# ❦ Brownies

1 c. sugar
¼ c. unsalted butter, melted
1 egg
2 oz. bittersweet Baker's chocolate, melted
¾ tsp. vanilla
½ c. flour

Mix ingredients in order given. Spread mixture evenly in buttered square baking pan. Bake at 350°F for 25–30 minutes. Turn out and cut in squares to serve.

*Variation:*
Add ½ c. chopped walnuts.

# ❦ Honey Brownies

*These are a rather dry variety of cookie that should be eaten soon after baking. They taste mostly of honey, so if you prefer a more chocolate-rich confection, double the amount of chocolate used.*

½ c. honey
⅓ tsp. baking soda
⅓ c. unsalted butter, softened
1 egg, well beaten
1 square bittersweet Baker's chocolate, melted
1⅔ c. flour
¼ tsp. salt
⅔ c. raisins
⅔ c. walnuts, chopped

Warm honey slightly but do not let it get hot. Add baking soda and butter; beat well. Add egg and chocolate, then sift in flour and salt. Lastly, add the nuts and raisins, slightly floured. Stir until stiff, adding more flour if necessary. Spread in buttered 9x12-inch baking pan and bake at 350°F for about 25 minutes, taking care not to let dry out. Cool and cut in squares to serve.

# ❦ Wheatless Fudge Bars

*Yet another example of the farmer's wife's wartime ingenuity.*

1 c. sugar
¼ c. unsalted butter, softened
2 eggs, separated
½ c. unsweetened cocoa powder
¼ c. barley flour
¼ c. rice flour
¼ tsp. salt
1 tsp. vanilla
½ c. walnuts, chopped

Cream sugar and butter; add egg yolks and cocoa powder. Sift in flours and salt; add to butter mixture. Beat egg whites till stiff with vanilla and fold into batter. Bake in a well-buttered 8-inch-square baking pan at 350°F. When done, cut into bars 1 inch wide and 3 or 4 inches thick to serve.

## Cocoa Sticks

*H. R., Wisconsin*

½ c. unsalted butter, softened
1 c. sugar
2 eggs
1 c. flour
3 tbsp. unsweetened cocoa powder
2 tbsp. milk
1 tsp. vanilla

Cream butter and sugar, then add eggs. Sift together flour and cocoa; add alternately with milk to butter mixture. Lastly add vanilla. Bake in a large, shallow, buttered pan at 400°F for about 30 minutes or until done. Cut in oblong sticks to serve.

# ❦ Chocolate-Nut Sticks

Woman's Home Companion *for December*

*A slight variation on the preceding recipe.*

1 c. sugar
¼ c. unsalted butter, melted
1 egg
2 squares bittersweet Baker's chocolate, melted
¾ tsp. vanilla
½ c. flour
½ c. walnuts, chopped

Mix all together. Line a 7-inch-square pan with buttered wax or parchment paper and spread mixture evenly in pan. Bake at 325°F until done. As soon as bars are removed from the oven, turn from pan and remove paper. Then cut in strips, using a long, sharp knife. If these directions are not followed, the paper will cling to cookie, then it will be impossible to cut it in shapely pieces. Roll in confectioner's sugar, if desired.

# ARE YOU A GOOD COOK?
## The Country Kitchen Starts a Correspondence Cooking Clinic

*March 1937*

**W**ell now, are you? A really good cook? Of course your family votes "yes," but you yourself are the severest critic. Let's get a little personal and see if we are satisfied with our cooking results, say 75 percent of the time.

I'm willing to wager that some of the very best cooks, especially those who have learned to cook by "rule of thumb," and by the looks and "feel" of a batter, don't always have good "luck" with modern recipes. Many young cooks excuse results with "well it tastes good anyway."

What are the most frequent causes of failure in following recipes? We consulted 20 famous Home Economists, trained women who put on hundreds of demonstrations who answer literally thousands of letters and talk to hundreds of thousands of homemakers each year. They are the originators and testers and demonstrators of many of your most useful and helpful recipes. Their *business* is to make cooking successful and easy. And here is what they give as the biggest cause of mortality in recipes:

*Failure to read a recipe carefully and to follow the method exactly.* Mentioned again and again were failure to measure accurately, poor equipment, and failure to sift flour once before measuring. Hmm! It's like hearing the ABCs again!

But wait. They don't mean fussy eighth-teaspoons and much sifting from this bowl to that. It's because they know so *much* about cooking and baking that they appreciate cause and effect.

Do you know how much difference it makes in a 3-cup flour recipe whether you sift the flour once before measuring, or whether you just dip the cup in the bin?

Look at our picture above, taken in our Country Kitchen. One Home Economics consultant says, "If a woman just *won't* sift flour before measuring, I tell her to stir it in the cup, then level it off." Practically all modern baking recipes call for flour sifted once before measuring.

*As noted at the beginning of this book, most flours these days are pre-sifted before packaging, so sifting before measuring is no longer necessary.*

# ❦ Apple Oat Bars

*Adapted from* Favorite Recipes of the King's Daughters and Sons

½ c. unsalted butter, softened

1 c. sugar

2 eggs

1 c. flour

1 tsp. baking powder

½ tsp. baking soda

½ tsp. salt

1 tbsp. unsweetened cocoa

1 tsp. cinnamon

½ tsp. nutmeg

¼ tsp. ground cloves

1 c. rolled oats

1½ c. apples, cored, peeled, and diced

½ c. walnuts, chopped

Cream butter and sugar; add eggs. Sift in dry ingredients, add apples and walnuts, and pour into buttered 9x12-inch baking pan. Bake at 375°F about 25 minutes. Cut in bars to serve.

## ❧ Banana Bars

*Adapted from* Favorite Recipes of
the King's Daughters and Sons

½ c. unsalted butter, softened
1 c. sugar
2 eggs
1 c. sour cream
2 ripe bananas, mashed
1 tsp. vanilla
2 c. flour
1 tsp. salt
1 tsp. baking soda
confectioner's sugar and
　chopped walnuts,
　　for sprinkling

Cream butter and sugar; add
eggs, then sour cream, bananas,
and vanilla. Mix well. Sift in dry
ingredients and mix. Pour into
buttered jelly-roll pan and bake
at 350°F for about 20 minutes.
Cool and cut in bars, then dust
with confectioner's sugar and
nuts to serve.

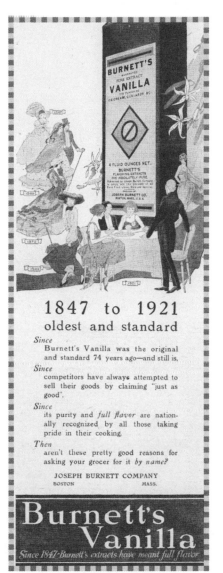

# Cocoanut Apricot Squares

*Adapted from* Cohasset Entertains

1 c. flour
1 tsp. baking powder
pinch salt
½ c. plus 3 tbsp. unsalted butter, softened
1 tbsp. milk
2 eggs, separated, plus 1 whole egg
1 c. apricot filling (see pg. 117)
1 c. sugar
2 c. unsweetened shredded cocoanut
1 tsp. vanilla

Sift together flour, baking powder, and salt. Work in ½ c. butter, then add milk and whole egg. Spread mixture into buttered 9x12-inch baking pan. Spread with apricot filling. Mix egg yolks with sugar, remaining butter, cocoanut, and vanilla. Spread over preserves. Beat egg whites till light; spread over top. Bake at 350°F for about 30 minutes. Cool and cut in squares to serve.

# ❧ Frosted Creams

| | |
|---|---|
| ⅓ c. unsalted butter, softened | ½ tsp. baking soda |
| ½ c. sugar | 2 tsp. baking powder |
| 1 egg | ½ tsp. cinnamon |
| ½ c. molasses | ½ c. buttermilk |
| 1½ c. flour | |

Cream butter with sugar; add egg. Mix in the molasses. Sift in dry ingredients, adding alternately with the buttermilk. Spread in buttered 9x12-inch baking pan and bake at 350°F till cooked through. Cool and frost with:

1 egg white
⅛ tsp. cream of tartar
1 c. sugar
⅓ c. water

Beat egg white with cream of tartar till stiff. Boil sugar with water till it spins a thread (230–234°F on a candy thermometer). Pour slowly over egg white and beat until smooth. Spread over cookie and cut in squares to serve.

# ❦ Frosted Almond Squares

*Adapted from* The Pennsylvania Dutch Cook Book

½ c. unsalted butter, softened

½ c. sugar

3 egg yolks

1 tsp. orange extract

1 c. flour

½ tsp. baking powder

½ c. blanched, slivered almonds

1 tbsp. orange rind

Cream butter and sugar, then add the egg yolks and extract. Sift in the flour and baking powder and mix well. Dredge ⅔ of almonds in a little flour and add to batter with orange rind. Pour into buttered baking pan. Bake at 350°F for about 20 minutes, till done. Cool and frost as for Frosted Creams (pg. 177). Sprinkle remaining almonds on top.

# Frosted Nut Cookies

½ c. unsalted butter, softened
1 c. sugar
2 eggs, well beaten
½ tsp. vanilla
1½ c. flour
½ tsp. salt
1 tsp. baking powder
1 c. walnuts, chopped

Cream butter; add sugar and mix together well. Add eggs, vanilla, and flour sifted with salt and baking powder. Spread ¼-inch thick on buttered baking sheet. Sprinkle with chopped nuts and frost with:

1 egg white
1 c. brown sugar
½ tsp. vanilla

Beat egg white till stiff, then fold in sugar and vanilla. Spread over cookie and bake at 375°F for 20 minutes. Cut in squares before entirely cool.

# ❦ Frosted Honey Fruit Cookies

*B. N., Nebraska*

½ c. unsalted butter, softened
1 c. brown sugar
1 egg
½ c. honey
2½ c. flour
1 tsp. baking soda
½ tsp. salt
1 tsp. cinnamon
¼ tsp. allspice
¼ tsp. ground cloves
½ c. buttermilk
¼ c. raisins, dredged in a little flour
1 c. walnuts, chopped
¼ c. unsweetened shredded cocoanut

Cream butter and sugar; add egg and honey. Sift in flour, baking soda, salt, and spices, adding alternately with buttermilk; then add raisins, nuts, and cocoanut. Mix all together well and spread thinly in two well-buttered 8-inch-square baking pans. Bake at 375°F for about 20 minutes. While still warm, frost with:

½ c. confectioner's sugar
milk to make a thin, smooth paste
few drops vanilla

Spread thinly over cookie and allow to cool. Cut in squares or diamonds to serve.

## ❦ Apricot Bars

*Adapted from* Cooking Favorites of Vergennes

1 c. flour
¼ c. sugar
½ c. unsalted butter, softened

Sift flour with sugar. Cut in butter until the mixture resembles coarse meal. Turn into a buttered 9-inch-square baking pan. Bake at 350°F for about 25 minutes. Top with:

2 eggs
1 tsp. vanilla
1 c. brown sugar
⅓ c. flour
½ tsp. baking powder
½ tsp. salt
1 c. dried apricots, finely chopped
½ c. pecans, finely chopped

Beat eggs with vanilla and mix in brown sugar. Sift in flour, baking powder, and salt, then add apricots and nuts. Spread over cookie, then return to oven for about 30 minutes. Cool and cut in bars to serve.

## 🌾 Apple Oatmeal Torte

| | |
|---|---|
| 1 c. flour | ½ c. brown sugar |
| ½ tsp. salt | ½ c. unsalted butter, melted |
| ½ tsp. baking soda | 1 egg |
| 1 tsp. cinnamon | 1 tsp. vanilla |
| 1½ c. rolled oats | 3 sour apples, cored, peeled and sliced |

Sift together first four ingredients, then mix in oats, sugar, butter, egg, and vanilla. Press half the mixture into a buttered 9-inch-square baking pan and arrange apple slices over it. Roll out remaining dough and press lightly over apples. Bake at 350°F for 25–30 minutes, till done. Cool and cut in bars to serve.

## 🌾 Lemon Bars

*Adapted from* The Meetinghouse Cookbook

| | |
|---|---|
| 2¼ c. flour | 4 eggs |
| ½ c. confectioner's sugar, | 2 c. sugar |
| plus more for dusting | ⅓ c. lemon juice |
| 1 c. unsalted butter, softened | ½ tsp. baking powder |

Sift together 2 c. flour and confectioner's sugar. Cut in butter, then press dough into buttered 9x13-inch baking pan. Bake at 350°F for 20–25 minutes, until just done. Beat together eggs, sugar, and lemon juice. Sift in remaining flour and baking powder and mix well. Pour over cake and return to oven for an additional 25 minutes. Dust with confectioner's sugar and cool. Cut in bars to serve.

# ❧ Nut Squares

| | |
|---|---|
| 1½ c. flour | 1 tsp. baking powder |
| ¼ c. sugar | ½ c. unsalted butter, softened |
| ¼ tsp. salt | 2 egg yolks |

Sift together dry ingredients, then cut in butter. Mix in yolks until smooth. Spread in buttered 8-inch-square baking pan and top with:

2 egg whites
1 c. brown sugar
½ c. shredded unsweetened cocoanut
½ c. walnuts, chopped
confectioner's sugar, for dusting

Beat whites stiff, gradually adding brown sugar. Add cocoanut and nuts and mix well. Pour over dough. Bake at 350°F for about 40 minutes. Cool, dust with confectioner's sugar, and cut in squares to serve.

# ❦ Creole Snacks

½ c. unsalted butter, softened
½ c. sugar
2 egg yolks
pinch salt
1½ c. flour
1 tsp. baking powder

Cream butter and sugar, add egg yolks, and mix well. Sift in dry ingredients. The mixture should be thick and crumbly. Pat into bottom of 9-inch-square buttered baking pan. Top with:

2 egg whites
½ c. sugar
¼ c. molasses
½ c. dates or raisins, chopped
½ c. shredded unsweetened cocoanut

Beat whites till stiff; add sugar gradually, then molasses, fruit, and cocoanut. Spread over cookie mixture. Bake at 350°F for 40–45 minutes. Cut in squares before serving.

*Variation:*
Substitute ¾ c. brown sugar for sugar in topping.

# ❦ Milk Chocolate Bars

*Adapted from* Cohasset Entertains

½ c. unsalted butter, softened       1¼ c. flour
½ c. brown sugar, packed           ¼ tsp. salt

Cream butter and sugar; sift in flour and salt. Mix well, then press into 9x12-inch buttered baking pan and bake at 350°F for about 20 minutes, till done. Sprinkle with:

8 oz. milk chocolate, grated or finely chopped
½ c. blanched almonds, finely chopped

Cool and cut in bars to serve.

# ❦ Chocolate Peanut Butter Bars

*Adapted from* Hot Recipes

⅓ c. unsalted butter, softened     ½ c. bittersweet chocolate,
¾ c. brown sugar                        grated or finely chopped
2 c. rolled oats                       ⅓ c. peanut butter
1 tsp. vanilla

Cream butter and sugar; add oats and vanilla. Spread onto buttered baking sheet and bake at 350°F for 8–10 minutes. Melt chocolate and add peanut butter, stirring till smooth. Spread over cookie when slightly cool. Cut in bars to serve.

# ❦ Apricot Bars

½ c. unsalted butter, softened
¼ c. sugar
1 c. flour

Mix butter, sugar, and flour and press into buttered 8-inch-square baking pan. Bake at 350°F for 15 minutes. Top with:

1 c. water
⅔ c. dried apricots
2 eggs
1 c. brown sugar
¼ tsp. salt
⅓ c. flour
½ tsp. baking powder
½ c. walnuts, finely chopped
½ tsp. vanilla

Cook apricots in water for 10 minutes, then drain, cool, and chop. Beat eggs, then add apricots and all remaining ingredients. Spread over cookie, then return to oven for an additional 30 minutes. Cool and cut in squares to serve.

# ❦ Pecan Bars

*Adapted from* Recipes from Maa Eway

½ c. unsalted butter, softened
1 c. sugar
1 egg
3 tbsp. heavy cream
1 tsp. vanilla
1¾ c. flour
2 tsp. baking powder
½ tsp. salt

Mix all ingredients together and spread in a buttered 8-inch-square baking pan. Top with:

2 egg whites, beaten stiff with
1 c. brown sugar
½ tsp. vanilla
½ c. pecans, chopped

Bake at 325°F for about 30 minutes. Cut in squares to serve.

# ❦ Filled Date Torte

Crumb mixture or streusel:
1½ c. flour
½ tsp. baking soda
½ tsp. salt
1 c. brown sugar
1½ c. rolled oats
1 c. unsalted butter, melted
1 c. walnuts, chopped

Sift together flour, baking soda, and salt, then mix in sugar and oats.
Add butter and nuts and mix thoroughly with the hands. Pat half of the
crumb mixture in a fairly shallow buttered baking pan. Top with:

Filling:
40 dates, chopped
1 c. water
1 c. sugar
½ tsp. vanilla

Cook filling until thick and smooth, add vanilla, then cool. Spread over
cookie, then add remaining crumb mixture, patting down well. Bake at
350°F for 45 minutes. Cool and cut in strips or squares to serve.

# ❦ Cheese Torte

1½ lbs. cottage cheese
8 egg yolks
3 tbsp. flour
1½ c. sugar
1½ c. heavy cream
⅛ tsp. salt
grated rind and juice of 1 lemon
1½ tbsp. butter, well creamed
8 egg whites, beaten stiff
fine breadcrumbs, for dusting

Mix in order given, folding in egg whites last. Bake in buttered 9x12-inch baking pan dusted with fine breadcrumbs at 350°F for 45 minutes. Cut in squares to serve.

# ❦ Raspberry Meringue Bars

*Meringue was a great favorite of the farmer's wife, allowing her to use up egg whites she might otherwise have discarded. This recipe using meringue is adapted from* The Meetinghouse Cookbook.

½ c. unsalted butter, softened
½ c. confectioner's sugar
2 egg yolks
1 c. flour

Cream butter and sugar, then add egg yolks. Sift in flour and mix. Press into unbuttered 9x12-inch baking pan and bake at 350°F for 10–15 minutes. Remove from oven and top with:

1 c. raspberry jam
2 egg whites
½ c. sugar
1 c. almond flour

Spread cookie with jam, then beat egg whites until stiff, gradually adding sugar. Fold in almond flour and spread over jam. Return to oven and bake 25 more minutes, till golden. Cool and cut in squares to serve.

# Gingerbread

## THE SECRET OF GOOD GINGERBREAD

By Jeanette Beyer and Eleanor Murray
*September 1930*

A good deal is to be said in favor of gingerbread. It is not only a simple sweet, which adds interest to a meal, but it will also furnish many economical and delicious calories, and there is abundant iron in its molasses to build bones and red blood.

If you have wondered at all the colors of gingerbreads, the black, the dark brown, the cinnamon, and all shades ranging to yellow, let me tell you the secret. Aside from molasses—of course the light or dark does make a difference—the leavening is the "x" in the recipe which accounts for the color variations. Since molasses and sour milk contain acid, soda is needed to neutralize and sweeten them, and this union of soda and acid produces the carbon dioxide gas (the same that comes from baking powder) which bubbles through the cake to make it light.

Now if you use very much soda, say two teaspoons in the recipe which I shall give you, your gingerbread will be very dark, of good volume, and flat on top. It will be wonderfully tender, but the texture will be coarse and the cell walls thick, because the excess soda has dissolved the thin walls. The flavor is fine, but slightly alkaline.

If you use just enough soda to neutralize the acid, about three-fourths teaspoon is added, the gingerbread will be good but not so large. The top will be rounded, the color lighter, and the texture not so coarse. But it will not be as tender as a cake, and will have more of the molasses flavor.

When no soda is added, but three teaspoons of baking powder used instead, the color is still lighter, the volume small and the texture fine. But the gingerbread will be tough and have a strong molasses flavor.

Three teaspoons of baking powder and sweet milk instead of sour milk will give about the same color, size and flavor as the gingerbread just above, but it is far tougher than any of the others.

So what does the gingerbread artist do? If she wants very dark tender cakes she uses soda, and for very light tough ones, baking powder. But for the perfect gingerbread, tender, mild in flavor, good texture and of medium color, she uses both baking powder and soda. Here is the recipe which can be mixed in ten minutes. You will go far to find a better:

## Perfect Gingerbread

2 c. flour

½ c. sugar

1½ tsp. ground ginger

½ tsp. cinnamon

2 tsp. baking powder

⅔ tsp. baking soda

¼ tsp. salt

¾ c. molasses

1 c. buttermilk

1 egg

¼ c. unsalted butter, melted

Sift all dry ingredients. Put wet ingredients in mixing bowl. Mix in dry ingredients and beat until smooth. Fill well-buttered shallow pan one-half full. Bake at 350°F, from 20 to 40 minutes depending on size. This makes a loaf 7½ inches square. Cut in squares.

The flour, as for all baking, should be sifted before measuring. An all-purpose flour is entirely satisfactory. If the molasses is very strong, sugar can be substituted for part of it. Instead of buttermilk, whey is good, and this same rule can be used with sweet milk, although the gingerbread will not be as tender.

With pungent molasses and spice, the flavor of the shortening is overcome so that drippings, lard, or any of the butter substitutes will make good gingerbread.

Probably there are hundreds of ways to serve gingerbread in all its varieties. Perhaps you have found how good it is hot with butter, or as a dessert topped by a fluff of whipped cream. Maybe you already vary it with nuts and raisins, or have tried adding ¾ c. cocoanut to the batter and sprinkling some over the top about 15 minutes before it is finished baking. Or maybe you eat it hot with lemon or hard sauce, or cover it with grated cheese and put the gingerbread in the oven long enough for the cheese to melt, serving it immediately.

*Following are some more variations on the Perfect Gingerbread recipe.*

Chocolate Gingerbread: Omit from recipe ½ c. flour and add 2 squares melted bittersweet Baker's chocolate. Ordinary gingerbread is also delicious iced with a fudge icing:

2 tbsp. unsalted butter, softened
1 egg
pinch salt
1 square bittersweet Baker's
    chocolate, melted
½ tsp. vanilla
2 c. confectioner's sugar
heavy cream as necessary

Beat first four ingredients until creamy. Add vanilla and sugar, along with enough cream to make an easy-spreading icing. Mix well and spread on gingerbread.

Tutti Frutti Gingerbread: To the batter, add 1½ c. chopped raisins, preserved ginger, dates, and orange peel mixed together. Cut in squares to serve.

Marshmallow Gingerbread: While gingerbread is still warm, split carefully in two layers and put three dozen large marshmallows between and on top. Put back in warm oven until soft, puffy, and golden brown. Cut in squares to serve.

Dutch Gingerbread: After spreading gingerbread mixture in pan, press into the top of it apples that have been pared, cored, and cut in thin slices. Sprinkle with sugar. Bake as above and cut in squares when cool.

Another Way with Apples: Pare, core, and slice several apples. Put in bottom of buttered square or oblong pan and sprinkle with sugar. A very little water may be added. Put in oven and start cooking. When just partially cooked, pour over a gingerbread batter, bake, cut in squares, and serve warm, with or without cream.

Maple Syrup Gingerbread: Substitute 1 c. maple syrup for sugar and molasses, and 1 c. sour cream for buttermilk.

# ❦ Composite Gingerbread

| | |
|---|---|
| ¼ c. sugar | ½ tsp. each cinnamon, |
| ⅓ c. molasses | nutmeg, and mace |
| ¼ c. unsalted butter, softened | 2 tsp. ground ginger |
| ¼ c. boiling water | ¼ tsp. salt |
| 1¼ c. flour | ¼ c. orange juice |
| 1½ tsp. baking powder | 1 tsp. orange rind, grated |
| ¼ tsp. ground cloves | 1 egg, beaten till light |

Mix sugar, molasses, and butter, then add water. Sift in dry ingredients, add orange juice and rind and, finally, the egg. Pour into buttered and floured 8-inch-square baking pan and bake at 350°F for about 40 minutes. Cool and top with:

| | | |
|---|---|---|
| ½ very ripe banana | 1 tsp. lemon juice | pinch salt |
| 1¼ c. confectioner's sugar | ½ tsp. vanilla | |

Mash banana with sugar till smooth, then add remaining ingredients and mix well. Spread over cookie and cut in squares to serve.

# PEACH GINGERBREAD

From *Peaches and Peaches* by Gertrude Shockey
*August 1928*

With peaches you can make many delicious and wholesome dishes. . . . Peach-topped gingerbread is best when eaten hot. Ingredients for the gingerbread: one cup brown sugar, one cup molasses, two even teaspoons of ginger, one teaspoon salt, three tablespoons butter, two eggs, one cup sour milk—or buttermilk—into which a teaspoon of soda has been dissolved, one teaspoon each of nutmeg and cinnamon, and a dash of allspice. Flour varies, but usually three cups are sufficient. Sift and gradually, using more or less as necessary, add the butter, melted, last. Batter should be rather stiff. Bake slowly, watching carefully, since any molasses dough burns readily. When done, frost with stiffly whipped cream dotted with eighths of rich ripe peaches that have been dipped in lemon juice to prevent discoloring.

# ❦ Lebkuchen (German Gingerbread)

*Mrs. D. K., Wisconsin*

*This German specialty, of medieval origin, is traditionally made with honey
and molded into shapes at Christmastime. Here is an uncharacteristically
soft, slightly chocolatey variation sent in by a* Farmer's Wife *reader.*

| | |
|---|---|
| 2 c. sugar | 3 c. flour |
| 6 egg yolks | 1 c. sweet milk |
| 1 c. molasses | 1 c. walnuts, chopped fine |
| 3 tsp. baking powder | peel of ¼ citron, chopped fine |
| 1 tsp. cinnamon | ¼ c. bittersweet chocolate, grated |
| ¼ tsp. ground cloves | 3 egg whites, beaten stiff |

Add sugar to egg yolks and beat well until light and fluffy. Stir in
molasses. Mix and sift the dry ingredients. Shake a little over the nuts
and citron. Add milk and flour mixture alternately to egg yolk mixture,
then add nuts, citron, and chocolate. Mix well, then fold in egg whites.
Spread in two buttered 9×12-inch baking pans. Bake at 350°F for 1
hour. Cool and ice with:

2 egg whites
1½ c. confectioner's sugar

Beat until quite stiff. Spread over gingerbread and cut in strips to serve.

## ❦ Bread Crumb Gingerbread

| | |
|---|---|
| 1 egg | 1 tsp. baking soda |
| ½ c. molasses | 1 tsp. ground ginger |
| 1½ c. breadcrumbs | ½ tsp. cinnamon |
| ½ c. buttermilk | ¼ tsp. salt |
| 1 c. flour | ¾ tbsp. unsalted butter, melted |

Beat the egg and add the molasses. Add the breadcrumbs, which have been soaked in buttermilk. Sift in dry ingredients, then add butter and mix thoroughly. Spread in large, buttered baking pan and bake at 350°F for about 30 minutes. Cut in squares to serve.

# ❦ Old English Gingerbread with Fruit Filling

*Mrs. H. E. C., Nebraska*

1 c. unsalted butter, softened
1 c. molasses
1 c. sugar
1 c. buttermilk
2 eggs
1 tbsp. ground ginger
3½ c. flour
1 tsp. cinnamon
1 tsp. baking soda
1½ tsp. nutmeg

Cream butter; add molasses and sugar. Add remaining ingredients and mix well. Bake in two 8-inch-square buttered baking pans at 325°F for about 30 minutes, until firm. Fill with:

1½ c. water (with a little grated lemon rind)
1 c. raisins
1 tbsp. lemon juice
¼ c. dried apricot pulp
½ c. sugar
1 tbsp. cornstarch
½ c. each walnuts, dried figs, and dates, chopped

Soak the raisins in the water, which has a little grated lemon rind in it. Marshmallows may be added, too. Add the rest of the ingredients. Cook until thick and spread between gingerbread layers. Ice or not, as preferred. Cut in squares to serve.

# Fried Treats

*The Farmer's Wife* made lots and lots of doughnuts over the years: for breakfast, for snacks, for special occasions and ordinary ones. They were an ample platform for her thrift; for frying she often used lard she had strained after a prior use. Vegetable oil is a reasonable—and inexpensive enough—substitute.

# DOUGHNUTS

By Annette C. Dimock
*March 1926*

*A doughnut and a cup o' tea,*
*A friendly chat twix't thee and me,*
*A pulse of heart in the busy day,*
*Lighten the load on the upward way.*

Every woman has her own recipe for making doughnuts, therefore, the variations for ingredients are many.

The number of eggs varies from one to three, or two egg yolks and one whole egg, or two whole eggs plus one extra yolk.

For shortening, sour cream, butter, chicken fat, lard, oil, or any sweet fat may be used.

From two-thirds to one cup of sugar to one cup of milk is the usual amount of sugar. Too much sugar or fat increases tendency to soak fat in frying.

Four to five cups of flour to one cup of milk may be used depending on the amount of fat in the dough. The less fat used, the softer the dough should be handled.

The following formulas may be used for raising the dough:

1 c. sweet milk:   1 tsp. soda plus 2½ tsp. cream of tartar
                   4 to 5 tsp. baking powder

1 c. sour milk:    ½ tsp. soda plus 2 tsp. baking powder

Flavors may consist of nutmeg, mace, or cinnamon, alone or mixed, one-fourth to one-half teaspoon of vanilla, lemon extract or grated rind of orange or lemon, one-half teaspoonful. One-fourth teaspoonful of ginger is often used with the supposition that it prevents soaking of fat in frying.

A doughnut with a soft crust and tender, cake-like texture that has a tendency to soak fat is made with three or four tablespoonfuls of fat, one cup of sugar, and two or three eggs. Another, of fine bread-like texture with firm, crisp crust that does not take up fat, calls for these ingredients:

2 eggs                ½ tsp. mixed spices
1 c. sugar            4 c. flour
2 tbsp. melted fat    1 c. sweet milk
4 tsp. baking powder  flour for rolling
1 tsp. salt

Beat eggs thoroughly, add sugar and beat vigorously. Add melted fat. Mix and sift together dry ingredients and add alternately with milk. Add flour to form soft dough. Put on floured board. Roll to one-fourth inch in thickness, cut out, and fry until golden brown. Turn as soon as they rise to the top of the fat and often during frying to give better shape.

Cut entire amount before beginning to fry cakes and allow them to stand a few minutes and rise and form a slight crust, which helps prevent soaking.

Potato doughnuts should be fried at once.

A chocolate doughnut may be made by adding one tablespoonful cocoa and one teaspoonful vanilla.

To ensure an even temperature of fat and to reduce chances of upsetting, a deep iron kettle with a bail is preferred. Fill with fat to nearly two-thirds its height. I prefer lard alone or two-thirds lard and one-third tried-out beef suet.

Fat should be hot enough to brown cubes of bread in one minute—never hot enough to brown them before they rise or so cool that they will soak fat.

If allowed to float, doughnuts require about three minutes to fry and about one and one-half minutes if submerged. However, for the woman who fried doughnuts often, a frying basket may prove a worthwhile investment, as the time for frying can be reduced to one-half and the fat absorption lessened. The quick process cannot be recommended, however, for large or thick doughnuts or for those that "swell shut."

After frying, strain fat through sieve over which cheesecloth has been placed. Wipe out kettle and return fat to it. With proper care, fat may be used many times with an addition of fresh fat as needed. The fat should never be overheated.

**Comforts:** Use standard rule with only two and one-half cups of flour. Add one cup raisins. Drop by spoonfuls into hot fat, fry to light brown, drain, and sugar.

**Sour Milk Doughnuts:** Omit fat in standard rule and substitute one-half cup sour milk [or buttermilk] and one-half cup thick, sour cream for the milk, or use one cup sour milk and one-half tablespoonful of fat.

**Bismarks or Jelly Doughnuts:** Roll dough very thin, cut with cooky cutter, and place a spoonful of marmalade or a few raisins in the center of each. Brush edge with cold water and cover with another round, pressing edges together.

To vary mixture, add to dough one-half cupful currants or raisins and two tablespoonfuls cut, candied citron and one-half teaspoonful of spice. Vary shape by cutting one-half-inch strips with a knife and twisting to form figure eight.

## ❦ Doughnuts

*Rebel*

3 eggs
1½ c. sugar
1½ c. sweet milk

1½ tsp. baking powder
1 tsp. salt
1 tsp. allspice

flour, enough so you can just handle on the board, patting instead of rolling out the dough

Mix well and roll out. Cut with doughnut cutter and cook in deep, hot fat. Drain on paper.

---

## ❦ Eggless Doughnuts

1 pint sweet milk
1 level tsp. salt
3 tbsp. lard, melted

1½ c. light brown sugar
2 rounded tsp. baking powder
flour

Mix slowly, since this slow mixing of flour is the secret of good doughnuts. Mix until stiff enough to roll out. Fry in deep, hot lard. Drain on paper.

## ❦ Nut Doughnuts

| | |
|---|---|
| 1 c. sugar | 2 tbsp. lard, melted |
| 1 c. mashed potatoes | pinch salt |
| 1 c. buttermilk | pinch each nutmeg and cinnamon |
| 2 egg yolks | ¼ c. walnuts mixed with 1 c. flour |
| ½ tsp. baking soda | more flour, to make a stiff dough |
| ½ tsp. baking powder | |

Stir together sugar and potatoes. Add remaining ingredients and mix all together. Roll out and cut in narrow strips. Fry in deep, hot fat. Drain on paper.

---

## ❦ Light Doughnuts

3 c. flour

3 heaping tsp. baking powder

½ tsp. nutmeg

¾ c. sugar

2 eggs, separated

1 c. milk

3 tbsp. unsalted butter, melted

Mix dry ingredients with egg yolks, milk, and butter, then beat egg whites stiff and fold in. Add more flour if necessary to make a soft dough—up to 2 c. more. Roll very thin, cut out, and fry in deep, hot fat. Drain on brown paper.

## Pumpkin Doughnuts

3 eggs, beaten light
1 c. sugar
1 c. sour cream
1 scant tsp. baking soda
pinch salt
2 tsp. cinnamon
1 tsp. nutmeg
1 c. pumpkin puree
4–6 c. flour, to make a rollable dough

Mix well and roll out ½ inch thick. Cut in strips, twist, and fry in deep, hot lard. While hot, roll in powdered sugar and cinnamon.

## Molasses Doughnuts

2 eggs
1 c. molasses
2 tbsp. shortening, melted
1¼ tsp. baking soda
½ tsp. salt
¼ tsp. nutmeg
¼ tsp. ginger
½ tsp. cinnamon
5 to 6 c. flour, sifted
1 c. buttermilk

Beat eggs and stir in molasses and shortening. Sift in baking soda, salt, spices, and 2 c. flour, adding to eggs alternately with buttermilk. Add more sifted flour to make a stiff dough. Roll out to ⅜ inch and cut in strips. Twist strips, fold in half, twist again, and pinch ends together. Fry in deep, hot fat. Drain on brown paper.

# Delicious Doughnuts

1 c. sugar
¾ c. sour cream
¼ c. buttermilk
3 eggs, beaten
1 tsp. baking soda
1 tsp. baking powder
½ tsp. nutmeg
½ tsp. salt
3½ c. flour

Add sugar to sour cream and buttermilk and let dissolve. Add eggs, then sifted dry ingredients to make a soft dough, adding a little more flour if necessary. Let stand 30 minutes. Fry in deep, hot fat. Fry enough at one time to make one layer on top of the fat and turn just once during frying. Drain on brown paper. Dust with confectioner's sugar if desired.

Gold Medal Doughnuts—
Lighter and better. One of
the delightful recipes constantly created in our kitchen.
Read our special offer.

# DEEP-FAT FRYING

By Mabel K. Ray

*March 1933*

The key to making wholesome fried foods is to have the fat at the correct temperature. That is, the fat must be hot enough when the food is put into it to form a crust on the food immediately so that grease will not be absorbed. Heat the fat gradually.

The sure way to get the right temperature is to use a thermometer. The second best method of testing temperature of fat is the bread cube test. An inch cube of bread cut from the middle of a slice is dropped into the deep fat. When a cube of bread turns brown in 60 seconds (335 to 360°F.), the temperature is right for [uncooked foods like doughnuts].

"But," you may say, "I was taught that when the fat started smoking it was hot enough to use for fat frying."

That is a serious mistake! For when fats smoke, they are not only hot enough to burn foods, but are themselves being broken down into substances which are irritating to the digestive organs. This is a permanent "break down" of the fat which can never be reclaimed—it is no longer the original fat but an entirely different chemical substance.

In order not to lower the temperature of the fat too much a small number of pieces should be fried at a time. The length of time the food should be cooked is determined largely by color. When the food is golden brown all over remove it and drain on absorbent paper.

"What kind of fat is best to use for deep frying?" That's a long story since there are so many excellent cooking oils and fats, including cottonseed, corn and other vegetable oils; lard and other animal fats. To be good for deep frying a fat should allow the food fried to keep its flavor and not give it its fatty taste. The fat should take up no flavors, it should heat to a high temperature without smoking or scorching, and it should be usable again.

Of the animal fats, lard is best to use for deep-fat frying. However, it smokes more quickly than the vegetable fats. The smoking temperature varies a good deal with the size of the vessel, the surface exposed, and the amount of foreign matter present. A deep iron or heavy aluminum kettle is best to use.

To clarify fat for further use, strain it through a cheesecloth while still warm. Raw potatoes may also be used. They should be cut into the cold fat and the fat heated gradually until the potatoes are browned. The foreign particles will settle to the bottom, then the clear fat liquid can be poured or skimmed off and stored in a covered jar in a cool place.

GOOD THINGS
TO EAT ARE
MADE WITH
BAKING SODA

## ❦ Grandmother's Crullers

2 c. sugar
4 eggs, or less if they are scarce
1 c. buttermilk
½ tsp. baking soda
4 to 6 c. flour, enough to make a smooth paste

Mix, roll out thin, and cut into 3-inch squares. Beginning half an inch from one end, cut the squares into three or four strips. Braid these, or twist them into fancy shapes, and fry in hot lard. Drain on paper and sprinkle with confectioner's sugar, if desired.

---

## ❦ Crullers II

*Adapted from* The Pennsylvania Dutch Cook Book

1 egg
1 egg yolk
1 c. sugar
1¼ tsp. baking soda dissolved in 1 c. buttermilk
4 c. flour
1 tsp. salt
1 tsp. cream of tartar
¼ tsp. cinnamon

Beat egg and yolk, add sugar, then buttermilk mixture. Sift in dry ingredients. Roll out thin on a floured board and cut with cutters. Fry in deep, hot fat and drain on brown paper.

# ❦ Sour Cream Crullers

⅓ c. butter
1½ c. sugar
1 small egg
pinch nutmeg
1 scant tsp. baking soda dissolved in ½ c. sour cream
2½ c. flour

Cream butter and sugar; add egg and nutmeg, then sour cream mixture. Add flour and mix well, adding more flour if necessary to make a dough that will roll out easily (it should be as soft as can be handled). Roll out to ¼ inch in thickness, shape with a cutter, and fry in deep, hot fat to a golden brown. Drain on thick brown paper for a moment and roll in confectioner's sugar while still warm. These crullers when properly made are not as liable to absorb the grease as a receipt in which more shortening is used.

YOU DON'T NEED TO WAIT FOR MILK TO SOUR TO BAKE WITH BAKING SODA

Squeeze 1½ tablespoonfuls of lemon juice into measuring cup.

Fill cup to the desired level with sweet milk.

Result—perfect liquid to use with ½ teaspoonful of baking soda in any baking soda recipe.

Tested
in the
Country
Kitchen

# ❦ Fattigmands

1 whole egg
5 egg yolks
6 tbsp. sugar
6 tbsp. heavy cream
1 tsp. extract (any type)
1¾ c. flour (enough to roll)

Beat egg and egg yolks, add sugar, then beat again. Whip cream and
add to eggs and sugar. Then add any type of extract and flour as for
cookies. Roll extremely thin and cut in diamond shapes. Make slit in
one point and slip end through. Fry in hot lard (they will fry very fast).
Turn as they come up and take out. Dust with powdered sugar if
you desire.

# ❦ Banana Fritters

*L. S., Nevada*

4 large, firm bananas
confectioner's sugar
lemon juice
1 c. flour
½ tsp. salt
2 eggs
⅔ c. milk

Remove banana skins, then cut in halves lengthwise and crosswise.
Sprinkle each piece with confectioner's sugar and a little lemon juice
and let them stand for an hour. Have ready a well-beaten batter made
of remaining ingredients. Dip bananas into this, fry in hot, deep fat, and
drain on brown paper.

## ❦ Apple Fritters I

1⅓ c. flour
2 tsp. baking powder
¼ tsp. salt
⅔ c. milk
1 egg, well beaten
2 medium-sized sour apples, peeled, cored, and thinly sliced

Mix and sift dry ingredients, then add milk and egg gradually. Stir in apples. Drop by spoonfuls and fry in deep fat. Drain well.

---

## ❦ Apple Fritters II

2 eggs, separated
½ c. honey
1 c. sour cream
2 c. flour
½ tsp. nutmeg
½ tsp. salt
½ tsp. baking soda
1 tbsp. unsalted butter, melted
4 sour apples, peeled, cored and sliced into ¼-inch rings

Beat egg yolks and honey till smooth, then mix in sour cream. Sift in flour, nutmeg, salt, and baking soda, then stir in butter. Beat egg whites till stiff and fold into batter. Dip apple rings in the mixture and fry in deep, hot fat, turning once to brown on both sides. Drain on brown paper.

# ❦ Funnel Cakes

*Adapted from* The Pennsylvania Dutch Cook Book

4 c. milk
4 eggs
½ tsp. baking soda dissolved in 1 tsp. water
2 tbsp. sugar
4 c. flour, approximately
pinch salt

Mix ingredients using enough flour to make a batter that will run smoothly through a funnel (hence, the name!) into deep, hot fat. Twist and turn funnel to make shapes. Drain on brown paper.

## ❧ Jolly Boys

| | |
|---|---|
| 1 c. flour | 3 tsp. baking powder |
| 2 c. rye flour | 1 egg |
| ⅓ c. fine cornmeal | 1 tbsp. molasses |
| ¼ tsp. salt | 1⅓ c. cold water |

Sift together flours, cornmeal, salt, and baking powder. Beat egg with molasses and 1 c. water. Add to first mixture and mix well. Add more water if necessary to make a stiff batter. Drop by the spoonful in deep, hot fat. Drain on brown paper.

--------------------------------------------------

## ❧ Snowballs

*Mrs. Tschida*

2 egg yolks
1 tbsp. heavy cream
few drops vanilla
pinch salt
1 tsp. cider vinegar
1 tsp. confectioner's sugar, plus extra for dusting
flour to stiffen—approximately to 2 c.

Blend yolks, cream, and seasonings. Add flour to stiffen. Roll out on floured board and cut in 1-inch circles. Drop in hot fat to cover, and with fork, lift up points as the ring fries to make it like a rosette. Fry a very light brown, drain, and sprinkle powdered sugar over to serve.

# ❦ Danish Snowballs

*J. D. C., California*

2 tbsp. butter, melted
2 c. flour
1½ c. boiling water
5 eggs
oil for frying

Add flour to butter, then add boiling water and stir over a medium-low flame until mixture forms a thick, smooth paste. Take from fire and cool. Beat in eggs, one at a time; beat hard for 10 minutes. With a teaspoon, form dumplings and drop in deep, hot fat. Cook until deep golden. Put on brown paper to drain. Serve hot with powdered sugar.

# Bibliography

Davidson, Alan. *The Penguin Companion to Food.* New York: Penguin Books, 2002.

Certain recipes in this book, as noted, were adapted from the following cookbooks:

*American Cooking: New England.* New York: Time-Life Books, 1970.

Berolzheimer, Ruth, ed. *United States Regional Cook Book.* Garden City, NY: Garden City Publishing, Inc., 1939.

*Cohasset Entertains.* Cohasset, MA: The Garden Club of Cohasset, 1979.

*Cooking Favorites of Vergennes.* Vergennes, VT: Students Going to Europe, date unknown.

*Favorite Recipes of the King's Daughters and Sons.* Chautauqua, NY: International Order of the King's Daughter's and Sons, 1978.

*Hot Recipes.* Georgia, VT: Georgia Firewoman's Auxiliary, date unknown.

Hutchinson, Ruth. *The Pennsylvania Dutch Cook Book.* New York: Harper & Brothers, 1948.

*The Meetinghouse Cookbook.* Concord, MA: Women's Parish Association, 1974.

*Our Favorite Recipes.* Metuchen, NJ: Women's Guild of the Presbyterian Church, date unknown.

*Out of Vermont Kitchens.* Burlington, VT: Women of St. Paul's Cathedral, 1999.

*Recipes from Maa Eway.* Evening Department Women's Club of Mahwah Cook Book Committee, 1958.

*Recipes Tried and True by Cooks.* Windsor County, VT: Members of the Home Demonstration Clubs of Windsor County, 1941.

Soper, Musia, ed. *Encyclopedia of European Cooking.* London: Spring Books, 1962.

# Index